Sweet Nothings

Sweet Nothings

HANDMADE CAMIS, UNDIES & OTHER UNMENTIONABLES

Valerie Van Arsdale Shrader

LARK BOOKS

A Division of Sterling Publishing Co., Inc.

New York / London

Art Director
Dana Irwin

Editor
Nathalie Mornu

Illustrator
Bernadette Wolf

Photographer
Lynne Harty

Cover Designer
Celia Naranjo

Library of Congress Cataloging-in-Publication Data

Shrader, Valerie Van Arsdale.
  Sweet nothings : handmade camis, undies & other unmentionables / Valerie Van Arsdale Shrader. -- 1st ed.
    p. cm.
  Includes index.
  ISBN 978-1-60059-383-3 (hc-plc concealed spiral : alk. paper)
  1. Lingerie. I. Title.
  TT670.S57 2009
  646.4'204--dc22

                              2009000814

10 9 8 7 6 5 4 3 2 1

First Edition

Published by Lark Books,
a Division of Sterling Publishing Co., Inc.
387 Park Avenue South, New York, NY 10016

Distributed in Canada by Sterling Publishing,
c/o Canadian Manda Group, 165 Dufferin Street
Toronto, Ontario, Canada M6K 3H6

Distributed in the United Kingdom by GMC Distribution Services,
Castle Place, 166 High Street, Lewes, East Sussex, England BN7 1XU

Distributed in Australia by Capricorn Link (Australia) Pty Ltd.,
P.O. Box 704, Windsor, NSW 2756 Australia

If you have questions or comments about this book, please contact:
Lark Books
67 Broadway
Asheville, NC 28801
828-253-0467

Manufactured in China

ISBN 13: 978-1-60059-383-3

For information about custom editions, special sales, or premium and corporate purchases, please contact the Sterling Special Sales Department at 800-805-5489, or specialsales@sterlingpub.com.

Contents

evening delicacies

sugar and spice

It's fun being a girl.

And sometimes the things that make being a girl so much fun are nothing much—a bit of lace, a tiny ruffle, a wisp of silk—yet those very little things can be ripe with deliciousness. Every one of us has a special drawer where these small wonders reside, and it is likely a feast for the senses, full of color and texture as well as charm and a little mystery, too.

When you choose the right garment to fit your mood, you know it: it's that little bit of lingerie that makes you feel beyond beautiful every time you wear it. *Sweet Nothings* offers you an entire collection of playful, sassy, sensual pieces that will sprinkle a little sugar into your day (and night). You can easily fill up your special drawer with lingerie of your own making—in your favorite colors, and sized just to fit you—and you'll be delighted at how simple and pleasurable it is to make your own dainty things.

A group of the best indie fashion designers share their designs in these pages; many of them specialize in lingerie only and are offering their secrets here. You'll find everything from lacy low-rise panties and sexy camisoles to pretty slips and seductive negligees. Whether you're looking for a robe for the morning, a silk

and everything nice

romper for lazing about the afternoon, or a garter belt to inspire some evening desire, you'll find a sumptu-ous offering of styles to fit your mood. Who can resist a tanga in stretchy lavender lace? Succumb to a tease of a chemise that doubles as a sundress. Fall under the spell of an absolutely adorable pair of polka-dot bloomers or a shimmering silk bustier. Perhaps you'd like to start by transforming a garment you already own. All it takes is a vintage slip or two to make a silky wrap skirt, a flirty nightgown, or a pretty brassiere. A perfect two dozen designs await your perusal; curl up and spend some time with each and every one.

A thorough introduction to the special techniques used in making lingerie and illustrated instructions will guide you through the projects, and as a bonus, you'll find full-size patterns for 15 of them, so you can make your favorite designs again and again.

Why are sweet nothings called sweet nothings? Wispy though they may be, those little items of lingerie are full of promise. Sugar or spice? Sassy or nice?

With *Sweet Nothings*, you decide.

how do I make thee?

do you love fabulous lingerie? It's so simple to sew all the delicious confections and saucy undies your heart desires. After all, intimate apparel usually calls for only a snippet of fabric and a few seams. Even if you're fairly new to sewing, you'll discover you have what it takes to make what you want, including the most extraordinary items (and without the extraordinarily high price).

The special allure of making lingerie is giving it your own style. If you wish to banish the basic panty from your life, for example, you can go custom all the way and sew your own from one-of-a-kind prints, amazing stretch laces, and sleek spandex knits. Try your hand at a tanga, tap, or low-rise panty. Make a matching camisole if you like. With your first attempt, you'll be addicted, and then you can make multiples to your heart's content.

Add a few more seams and you can make a wardrobe of nighties and jammies for lounging, sleeping, and … other times. You'll find something sweet to satisfy all your whims: Cut apart a 1970s mod print bed sheet to make a cheeky chemise with retro style. Give classic nylon tricot the goddess treatment by ruching simple, straight fabric pieces into a baby doll look like the one on page 42. Ruffle the edges of organic cotton knit fabric to infuse sleep separates with an au naturel attitude. Or take two vintage slips, dye them, layer them, and add some trimmings for charm in the boudoir.

For snug wraps and cover-ups, exercise your freedom to use luscious fabrics in yummy prints you simply won't find in shops. With a few basic body measurements to guide the way, for instance, you can make an exotic kimono in an unexpected sheer fabric. Go glam with a caftan in printed chiffon and add bling to the neckline with beaded trim. Choose seductive silk dupioni for a form-fitting bustier that blurs the line between what you might wear in private and what you can wear in public. A bra is just as easy to make as anything else. Just base it on a pair of round doilies, a vintage full slip, or some stretchy lace, and watch the cup shapes develop naturally as you add the finishing touches.

As tempting as it is to keep the lingerie you make, the breezy delicates in this book also make great gifts. A sure way to spice up any bridal shower or birthday party is to surprise a special friend or favorite relative with a sweet nothing you've created entirely on your own, just for her.

Delicious Fabrics

You know that lingerie is all about the fabric and how it makes you feel. Are you in the mood for a little cotton tank today, or a lacy camisole? Many fabrics can be used for lingerie. From shiny spandex knit to filmy woven voile, as long as you find it irresistible, almost any fabric that's soft, lightweight, fluid, and caresses the skin, will work.

The one practical detail you'll need to keep in mind is whether or not the fabric stretches. Knit fabrics usually stretch, while woven ones don't, although there are exceptions in both categories. Often the stretch factor is the key to the body-hugging style or self-adjusting fit of a lingerie design. On the other hand, the floating, lighter-than-air quality of a non-stretch fabric might be the best choice for something loosely fitted and flowing. In *Sweet Nothings*, the project directions will tell you what kind of fabric each designer used, and help you answer the stretch question with confidence.

Whether or not you're looking for the stretch factor, there are many sources for desirable fabrics. When you shop in traditional fabric stores, be sure to check out the bridal and eveningwear sections, where you'll find plenty of lustrous

options such as crepe-backed satin and silk dupioni, plus lace, chiffon, and other sheers. Browse the aisles displaying sports and swimwear fabrics to find soft cotton jersey and sleek spandex knits. Most lingerie projects require just a small amount of cloth, so you may find some bargains waiting for you on the remnant table as well.

Surf the Web, too, to find lingerie fabrics and related materials. Online sources offer an amazing selection of fabrics in solid colors, stripes, and exotic prints. You can usually download or request a catalog for easy browsing and order sample swatches at a nominal price before placing an order.

You can also adapt and alter treasures you uncover in thrift shops, flea markets, and estate sales for imaginative reuse as lingerie. Vintage finds such as embroidered linen tablecloths, doilies, printed bed sheets, and old-fashioned full-length slips are used as the "fabric" for several projects in this book. Borrow them as inspiration for your own unique creations.

YUMMY FABRIC CHOICES

Here's an inside peek at the fabrics most often used by the designers for the projects in this book.

batiste

Batiste is a fine, soft, semi-sheer fabric woven from pure cotton or cotton blends. While it's often chosen for heirlooms like christening gowns for infants and smocked dresses for little girls, it also makes great grown-up lingerie. It's available in 45-inch (1.1 m) and 54-inch (1.4 m) widths in white and pastels.

chiffon

Chiffon is a soft, transparently sheer fabric woven from silk or polyester fibers. Usually 45 inches (1.1 m) wide, this ultra-feminine fabric comes in prints and a great number of solid colors.

satin

Crepe-backed satin is also known as satin-backed crepe because the fabric has two distinct faces. One has the matte finish and pebbly texture of crepe, while the other has a smooth, satin sheen. The fabric has a weighty feel with a very luxurious drape. Usually available in a 45-inch (1.1 m) width when made from silk or a generous 58-inch (1.5 m) width when made from polyester, this fabric comes in a wide range of solid colors.

silk

Dupioni silk, typically 45 inches (1.1 m) wide, is a supple, crisp, lustrous fabric woven from uneven threads that create an interesting nubby texture. Because silk is so easy to dye, dupioni comes in countless solid colors. Synthetic look-alikes may be made from polyester or acetate.

knits

Jersey is a lightweight knit, similar to a T-shirt. It stretches more across the fabric than along its length. Jersey comes in cotton, including pure organic cotton, as well as fiber blends such as cotton/polyester and cotton/spandex. You can find jersey in solid colors, stripes, and prints. Some jerseys are 54 inches (1.4 m) to 60 inches (1.5 m) wide, while others are tubular and can be used, as is, to make quick and easy seamless camisoles.

Spandex knit is sometimes called two-way or four-way stretch knit because it gives greatly in all directions, typically 25 percent across the fabric and 75 percent along its length. This makes it perfect for lingerie such as panties, bras, and camisoles that are designed to fit like a glove. The nylon/spandex type is often called swimwear knit, while the cotton/

Wide stretch lace bridges the divide between fabric and trim. It looks like a trim because it's a lace with the long edges finished, usually in a scallop design. Because it's 4 to 7 inches (10.2 to 17.8 cm) wide and has elastic spandex fibers, it's sized just right for an easy-to-make panty, bra, or camisole. The finished edges streamline the sewing and the built-in stretch takes care of the fit. Once you've used this great material, you'll want to stitch it onto everything!

lace everyplace

spandex type may be called activewear knit, reflecting the common, non-lingerie uses for these knits. Spandex knits come in a wide selection of solid colors and prints and are usually 58 inches (1.5 m) wide.

Tricot is a lightweight knit that doesn't stretch, and it's a classic lingerie fabric. Some tricots have an anti-static, non-cling finish. Usually made of nylon, this fabric is strong, durable, and available in sheer and semi-sheer weights in many solid colors and prints. Because tricot is very wide—usually about 108 inches (2.7 m)—you can often cut multiple items from a single length.

voile

Voile means "veil" in French, which tells you a lot about this fine, soft, lightweight fabric that you can almost see through. Usually woven from pure cotton or cotton blends, this 50-inch-wide (1.3 m) to 60-inch-wide (1.5 m) fabric comes in solid colors, prints, and novel embroidered versions.

Crave luscious color? Create lingerie in the colors you love with easy-to-use household and craft dyes. This is also a clever way to make everything—fabric, straps, elastic, and trims—a custom match.

Simply choose the color of dye you're passionate about. Next, read the dye's label and follow the manufacturer's directions. For more information and some helpful tips, you can visit the manufacturer's website. The site may have recipes for combining standard dyes to make unique, vivid colors.

Chances are the equipment you'll need for dyeing is already on hand. For a container, use an old plastic, enamel, or stainless steel bowl or bucket. A long-handled plastic spoon will do for stirring and mixing, but reserve these items for dyeing only, because they will no longer be suitable for cooking. To prevent stains, it's a smart move to wear rubber gloves and cover the work surface with several layers of newspaper.

A heat treatment or a salt soak may be needed as a final step to set the color permanently. The dye label will tell you this, as well as anything else you need to know.

tame the wild beast

Slick, shiny fabrics make fabulous little nothings, but they can slip and slide as you handle them. Follow these tips to tame them:

- Often the wrong side of the fabric is less slippery than the right side, so fold the fabric with wrong sides together for pattern layout. Or lay out the pattern on a single layer of fabric.

- For a greater degree of control, cover the work surface with a matte material that has some "tooth" to resist the fabric's tendency to slide. For instance, you might use a bed sheet, a flannel-backed plastic tablecloth with the flannel side facing up, or a wool-like blanket. Use weights to hold the pattern steady during layout (you can purchase special sewing weights, or use household items such as small cans of food). Trace around the pattern with a fabric marker. Remove the weights and cut out the pattern along the traced outlines.

- Another option is to pin the fabric in a single layer to an underlay of paper. You might use brown kraft paper or sheets of tissue-weight wrapping paper taped together. Pin the fabric to the underlay, and then pin the pattern in place through both layers. Cut out the pattern through both the fabric and the underlay.

- Use a "with nap" layout that aims the tops of all the pattern pieces in one direction only—so the finished lingerie has a consistent luster. This is necessary because shiny fabrics look lighter in one direction, and darker in the other; sometimes the difference is subtle, but it will be noticeable in the finished lingerie.

- Use pins generously. More pinning than usual will help keep the fabric under control as you sew seams and hems.

- Prevent the fabric from being pulled down into the sewing machine throat plate by holding the bobbin and needle threads taut and slightly upward behind the presser foot as you start stitching. Also helpful is a straight stitch throat plate that has a smaller opening than the standard, all-purpose plate. If this plate isn't already one of your sewing machine accessories, you can purchase one from a sewing machine dealer.

Luscious Lace & Other Tasty Trims

What's lingerie without lace and other delicious trimmings? Whether you like a little bit of trim or prefer a more lavish treatment, personalize lingerie by choosing embellishments you find appealing and use them well and often.

LACE EDGING

Lace edging is often used for the projects in this book. This lace is sometimes called single edge lace because it has one fancy, scalloped long edge and one plainer, straight long edge. As you might guess from its name, this type of lace is used to trim lingerie along edges such as waistlines, leg openings, and hems. The plain edge of the lace is sewn to the lingerie, while the fancy edge hangs free.

A soft lace edging made from nylon or polyester fibers is perfect for lingerie because it feels good as it brushes against your skin, and it won't show as bumps through other garments you may wear over it. Although most lace edgings come in white, off-white, and black only, there are some fashion colors available. The colors may be matched to a favorite lingerie fabric such as tricot knit.

Various widths are available from narrow ⅜ inch (1 cm) and less to 12 inches (30.5 cm) and more. Narrow lace measuring about ½ inch (1.3 cm) wide is recommended for leg and armhole edges, and wider lace measuring about 1 inch (2.5 cm) is recommended for waistlines. For hems, almost any width you like can work. You could start with lace in the 2-inch (5.1 cm) to 3-inch (7.6 cm) range and go up or down from there to make the perfect choice.

Some soft lace edgings are stretch laces. These are an excellent and comfort-giving choice for lingerie edges that are fitted closely to your body, such as the lower edge of a camisole or the waist and legs of panties.

RIBBON

Ribbons come in almost any type you can imagine, from skinny to wide, shiny to matte, and plain to highly decorative. Some ribbons are even made from lace. For lingerie, ribbons are used to create straps, drawstrings, and, of course, trims. When a project calls for ribbon, the directions will tell you how much to buy and what width you need for the purpose the designer has in mind.

You can also purchase packets of tiny bows, rosebuds, butterflies, and similar accents made from narrow ribbon to use as finishing touches. Just a few hand stitches will put them in place. It's no secret that these little embellishments are also a great way to conceal any stitches that turned out less than perfectly.

BIAS BINDING

Bias binding, used mainly to finish raw fabric edges on lingerie by enclosing them, is woven fabric cut into strips, then folded and pressed. The strips are cut on the pliant bias grain of the fabric, which runs diagonally at a 45° angle from the selvage edge of the fabric. The bias grain is so stretchy that it will lie smoothly on curved and shaped edges as well as on straight edges.

Single-fold binding is formed when each long, raw edge of the bias strip is folded to the wrong side and pressed. For double-fold binding, the tape is then folded again, wrong sides together, with the long edges slightly offset. You can sew this binding to a lingerie edge with just a single row of machine stitching.

Double-fold bias binding can be purchased in various solid colors, prints, and metallics, or you can make it yourself from virtually any smooth, lightweight fabric. To make your own, cut bias strips of fabric four times the width you need, then fold and press the strips as described on page 32. A pressing aid called a bias tape maker (page 23) automatically folds under the long edges as you press, streamlining this first step wonderfully.

There are other ways to use bias binding. For example, you can make lingerie straps or a drawstring simply by stitching the long edges of the binding together.

Elastic & Other Notions

Elastic stretches and then recovers its original size, promising rewards of comfort and automatic, self-adjusting fit. Even though it's not so sexy, elastic is essential for many lingerie designs.

Elastic comes in many widths. Usually a ½-inch (1.3 cm) to 1-inch (2.5 cm) width is used for waist edges, while ¼ inch (6 mm) to ⅜ inch (1 cm) is used for leg, neckline, and arm-hole openings.

Of course, all elastics are not alike, something you'll want to keep in mind when selecting them. Although connoisseurs might savor the little differences between one elastic and another, what you really need to decide is whether you want elastic that's firm or soft, pretty or plain.

Elastics can be woven, plaited, or knitted, and these constructions make them either very firm and shape-retentive or quite soft and flexible. More often than not, gentle, soft-stretch elastic that's knitted or woven will make you happier with the completed lingerie project than a more rigid, plaited type. If the elastic hides behind the lingerie seams, such as in a fabric casing, then basic, plain elastic will do. When elastic is sewn along an edge and meant to show, choose special lingerie elastic that has one long decorative edge. Some of these elastics have a picot edge with lacelike open loops, some have a ruffled edge, and some have a plush backing that feels especially nice against the skin. And that's part of the point, isn't it?

BONING

Some say that vintage corsets, which molded the female body into fashionable, wasp-waisted shapes of the day, showcased the art of dressmaking in an extraordinary way. Whalebone stays (AKA boning), sewn into hidden fabric channels in contoured seams, were the dressmaker's trick for sculpting the figure's shape. Some of today's lingerie borrows from this tradition, though fortunately with a much lighter touch.

Among the easiest kind of modern boning to use is the ¼-inch-wide (6 mm) or ½-inch-wide (1.3 cm) plastic kind sold by the yard or in a package containing a precut length; you'll find it in the notions area of the fabric store. You can simply cut this boning with craft scissors to the length you need. Be sure to round off the boning tips with the scissors to remove any sharp edges that could poke through the lingerie fabric or dig into your skin. If the boning comes

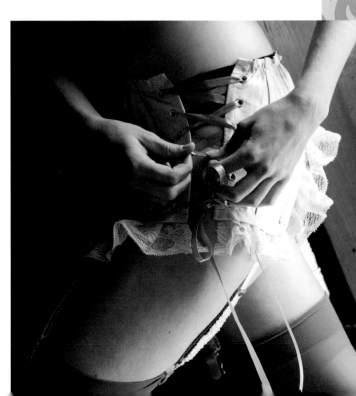

covered in fabric, slide the boning partially out of this sleeve to round off the tips. The projects in *Sweet Nothings* that call for boning will tell you how and where to sew the fabric channel that holds the boning in place.

HOOKS AND EYES

A concealed closure set consisting of a small metal hook and a loop-shaped metal eye is often used on lingerie. You sew these sets in place by hand (page 33).

A bra back is fabric tape with sets of hooks and eyes already sewn in place. The sets usually are spaced about ¾ inch (1.9 cm) apart to allow for fit adjustments at the center back of a bra. You can purchase bra backs in different widths with one, two, or three rows of hooks and eyes. You can also remove the bra back piece from an existing bra and recycle it when you sew.

GROMMETS

Grommets, like the ones in the garter belt on page 99, can add a whole new dimension to your lingerie—just *think* of the lace-up possibilities! Grommets may look intimidating, but they're really quite simple to install. Look for kits that contain setting tools, usually a special pair of pliers or a mallet, and just follow the instructions on the packet.

Bare Necessities

If you have some sewing experience, you probably have most of the tools and supplies you need to sew various kinds of lingerie. All of the projects in this book call for the Sewing Kit in the box below, so gather these items before you start. Read on for more about the essentials you'll need to have on hand before you craft your dainties.

SEWING TOOLS

You'll need a basic sewing machine that sews straight and zigzag stitches. If your model has settings for sewing a three-step zigzag stitch, a hemming stitch that combines a sequence of straight and zigzag stitches, a stretch stitch, and/or machine buttonholes, you'll find those settings helpful for a number of the projects in this book. A zipper foot—an accessory presser foot usually included with the purchase of a sewing machine—is also helpful for some of the projects.

When you start a new project, insert a fresh sewing machine needle to avoid stitch snafus. Match the needle size and type to the fabric. For example, if you're using a very thin, light-weight fabric such as tricot, chiffon, batiste, or voile, select a fine needle in size 8/60, 9/65, 10/70, or 11/75. To help sew smoothly on knits, go with a ballpoint or stretch needle in size 10/70 for lightweight jersey or 12/80 for spandex fabrics.

Sewing Kit

Sewing scissors or shears

Craft scissors (for paper)

Pinking shears (optional)

Tape measure

Straight pins

Safety pins for threading elastic

Hand-sewing needles

Thread to match your project

Embroidery needle, floss,
    and hoop (optional)

Seam ripper

Rotary cutter, mat, and ruler

Water-soluble fabric marker
    or chalk marker

Tissue/wrapping or kraft paper
    (for drawing patterns)

Pencil with an eraser

Iron and ironing board

Bias tape maker

Bodkin

Fray retardant

Tube turner

A serger, the household version of an industrial-style machine, is a useful supplementary machine that makes sewing lingerie seams and hems fast and easy. The serger has built-in blades that trim the fabric's raw edges while two, three, or more threads interlock to sew the stitches; it's the kind of stitching you'll see on lingerie you purchase in a retail shop. If the serger model can sew a cover stitch, has an attachment for applying elastic, and/or can make a rolled hem, you'll find these features helpful for several of the projects in this book. To select the best serger needle for lingerie, consult the machine's manual.

For the sewing machine, all-purpose pure polyester or polyester/cotton blend sewing thread suits most lingerie fabrics, and there's a wide range of colors to help you find a perfect match. If sewing on a thin or sheer fabric, extra-fine all-purpose thread is a better choice; it sews a finer seam, and without the puckers a standard-gauge thread can produce on delicate fabrics. For a serger, all-purpose polyester overlock thread is fine enough to produce a suitable seam on virtually any lingerie fabric used in this book.

Although almost all the stitching on lingerie is accomplished by machine, a few hand stitches are called for in some projects. For this, you'll need standard hand-sewing needles, called "sharps," in medium sizes from about 7 to 11. Needle packets containing assorted sizes are inexpensive and widely available, and they let you experiment a little to find the size you're most comfortable using. You'll also need a thimble that fits your finger.

CUTTING TOOLS

You can use common sewing tools such as small scissors for clipping threads and other detail work, plus a pair of shears for cutting fabric. Make sure the blades are sharp and clean; scissors and shears in good condition will slice through lingerie fabrics easily, and your cuts will be accurate.

You won't want to use a rotary cutter for sheer fabrics, but it's still an efficient tool for cutting cotton and vintage sheet fabrics. Always cut the fabric on a self-healing mat. The wide, transparent ruler designed for rotary cutters is also useful for marking angled cuts of 30°, 45°, and 60°.

Protect Your Pinkies

Rotary cutters are fast and sharp. Get in the habit of cutting away from yourself, while keeping your finger-tips out of harm's way. When you've finished cutting, always remember to engage the safety latch.

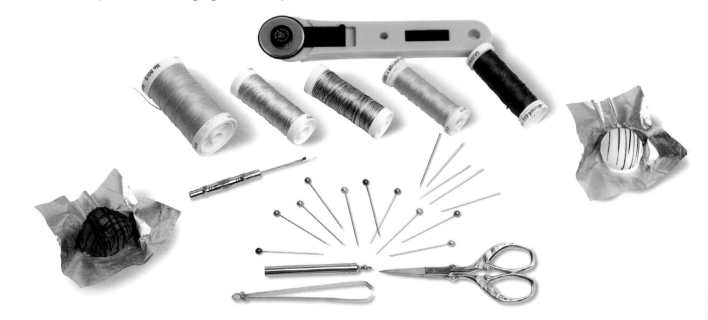

PRESSING TOOLS

Although there's minimal pressing when sewing lingerie, you do need an iron and ironing board. It helps to have an iron that allows low temperature settings and the option of using no steam for many of the more fine lingerie fabrics. A press cloth will help protect the fabric from heat. Always test the iron settings on fabric scraps first.

A typical lingerie seam has a narrow seam allowance pressed to one side. Use a light touch for this to avoid making imprints on the fabric.

OTHER NECESSITIES

A few additional tools and supplies will make your sewing experience much more pleasurable.

A bias tape maker is a time-saving pressing tool that helps you produce single-fold bias binding by folding the long, raw edges of fabric strips as you press. This tool comes in sizes that indicate the finished, pressed width of the bias tape: ¼ inch (6 mm), ½ inch (1.3 cm), ¾ inch (1.9 cm), 1 inch (2.5 cm), and 2 inches (5.1 cm). When making your own double-fold bias binding, select the tape maker that is twice the desired finished size of the binding, because you'll need to fold the pressed strip in half. For example, select a 1-inch (2.5 cm) tape maker to create ½-inch (1.3 cm) double-fold bias tape.

A bodkin helps you thread elastic or a drawstring through a narrow channel such as a casing. This tool has a large eye or clasp at one end and a blunt tip at the other to make the step quick and easy. You can substitute a safety pin for a bodkin.

A fabric marker creates temporary marks on fabric to help you get your bearings as you sew. A chalk marker or a pen with evaporating ink works well on lingerie fabrics. Test the marker on fabric scraps to make sure the marks are easy to remove without leaving permanent stains.

Fray retardant is a clear, alcohol-based liquid used to seal thread ends. A drop can be used to seal the end of a serger seam and prevent the stitches from unraveling.

A tape measure is necessary for taking body measurements. Select a plastic or plastic-coated fabric tape that won't stretch.

A tube turner streamlines the occasionally challenging step of turning a narrow fabric tube right side out, such as when making spaghetti straps. Many devices for turning fabric tubes are available. A practical, multipurpose choice is the standard 12-inch-long (30.5 cm) tool that has a latch hook at one end and a pull ring at the other. You can substitute a blunt hand-sewing needle.

Fetching Fit

Perfect fit is a private indulgence that's yours to savor when you sew your own lingerie. It's easy to finesse the fit because lingerie patterns are not at all complex, and there are often self-adjusting elements incorporated into the designs, such as stretch fabrics and elasticized edges.

To help you judge the fit, you can compare a lingerie pattern to a similar item already in your lingerie chest. Lay each part of the pattern over the corresponding area of the item, aligning the seams, to see whether you need to alter the pattern. (Don't forget to include the seam allowance.)

One of the beautiful things about *Sweet Nothings* is that the projects can be tailored to work for you, however you like things to fit: loose and comfy, snug and sexy, or somewhere in between. You won't have to experience that frustration of trying on a million bras before finding one that even remotely fits, or grabbing a pair of panties from the Small rack only to get home and discover there's a decided lack of stretch.

Some of the projects in this book virtually guarantee excellent fit because they begin with personal body measurements, and the pattern evolves from there. Other projects offer a choice from a range of sizes. To keep things on a level playing ground, we offer a general sizing chart that should serve as a basic guide for all the projects. The chart reflects a combination of the vanity sizing you find in most catalogs and the standard sizes that are used in most commercial patterns. With international designers and readers of all body types, we think this happy medium works especially well for handmade lingerie. To decide which size matches your figure, consult the chart at the top of page 25.

Not all the projects come in every single size, but most have instructions for three or four options. When necessary, full patterns are provided showing these options based on the measurements in our chart. But, depending on how you want the item to fit and the fabric you choose, you may want to go

	XS	*S*	*M*	*L*	*XL*
	Fits Sizes 2–4	Fits Sizes 6–8	Fits Sizes 10–12	Fits Sizes 14–16	Fits Sizes 18–20
Bust	32–34 inches (81.3–86.4 cm)	34–36 inches (86.4–91.4 cm)	36–38 inches (91.4–96.5 cm)	40–42 inches (101.6 cm–106.7 cm)	42–44 inches (106.7–111.8 cm)
Waist	24–26 inches (61–66 cm)	26–28 inches (66–71.1 cm)	28–30 inches (71.1–76.2 cm)	32–34 inches (81.3–86.4 cm))	34–36 inches (86.4–91.4 cm)
Hip	34–36 inches (86.4–91.4 cm)	36–38 inches (91.4–96.5 cm)	38–40 inches (96.5–101.6 cm)	40–42 inches (101.6 cm–106.7 cm)	44–46 inches (111.9–116.8 cm)

up or down a size. For instance, the Stargazer cami and panties on page 118 were created with satin spandex, and if you intend to wear them for swimming, you'll want to size them down. If you plan on lounging around the house, you'd probably size them up. You get the idea. With some projects, you'll use existing clothes as your starting point—vintage slips, a store-bought tank top, or your own favorite underwear, as a template. And for others you'll just take your own body measurements and go from there.

You may not want your lingerie to fit as tightly as we depict, or the reverse. Maybe you're in the mood for a really snug fit. If you use the sizing chart, examine the patterns, and review the instructions before you get started, you should have no problem adjusting the project so it fits just as you want it to.

Tantalizing Techniques

Nearly every stitch you'll take when creating lingerie is made by machine. Master these basic techniques to create quality underthings you'll love to wear.

SEAMS

For lingerie seams, use the seam allowance (the distance between the raw edge of the fabric and the seamline where you stitch) stated in the project directions. This will vary from ¼ inch (6 mm) to ⅝ inch (1.6 cm). Completed lingerie seams usually are narrow, so the directions often tell you to trim the seam allowance close to the stitching after you have finished sewing a seam.

Serged seams are perfect for lingerie, and the serger allows you to make seam allowances as narrow as ⅛ inch (3 mm)—and you can skip the step of trimming seam allowances by hand. Consult the serger manual to see which kind of seams your model can make, and learn which tension and stitch length adjustments you may need to make for good results on lingerie fabrics.

When sewing on a standard sewing machine, experiment on fabric scraps to see whether you must adjust the sewing machine for smooth stitching. You may find a shorter stitch length, for example, produces a seam that looks just right, especially on sheer fabrics.

double-stitched seam

As you might guess, this seam is made with two rows of stitches. It's the most common lingerie technique.

The first row of stitches goes on the seamline. Sew this row with ordinary straight stitches, or, when working with stretch knits, a medium-length, narrow-width zigzag stitch. Press the seam allowances to one side.

Place the second row of stitches in the seam allowance, ⅛ inch (3 mm) to a scant ¼ inch (6 mm) away from the first row.

You can use straight stitches, zigzag stitches, or a three-step zigzag stitch for the second row. Zigzag stitches prevent the seam allowances from curling on knits, and the three-step zigzag prevents lightweight fabric from tunneling. As a final step, trim the seam allowances close to the second row of stitches.

Another option for the second row is using a two- or three-thread serger stitch to overcast the seam allowances together and trim them automatically.

french seam

This seam, used on lightweight woven fabrics, completely encloses raw fabric edges and looks as polished on the wrong side as on the right side of lingerie. You will need a seam allowance of at least ⅝ inch (1.6 cm) to create this seam.

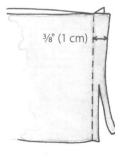

⅜" (1 cm)

figure 1

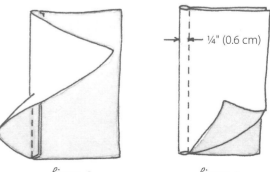

¼" (0.6 cm)

figure 2   *figure 3*

1

With wrong sides of the fabric facing, use a straight stitch to sew a ⅜-inch (1 cm) seam on the right side of the fabric. Trim away half of the seam allowance (figure 1).

2

Press the seam open, then fold with right sides facing. Press to make a crease along the stitch line (figure 2).

3

Stitch a ¼-inch (6 mm) seam on the wrong side, encasing the seam allowance. Open up the fabric and press the seam to one side (figure 3).

HEMS

Three kinds of machine-sewn hems are often used for the lovely lingerie projects in this book. Use the hem allowance (the amount of fabric folded up to form the hem) stated in the project directions.

topstitched

This neat and durable hem is easy to sew. Fold under the raw edge, then fold up the hem, and press. Sew straight stitches along the upper edge of the hem.

edgestitched

Another easy-to-sew hem, this technique creates a very narrow finish for fabrics that don't ravel. Simply fold up the hem, and press. Sew straight or short, narrow zigzag stitches close to the fold. Trim the hem allowance close to the stitches.

folded and edgestitched

This type of hem creates a very narrow finish with the raw edge enclosed. Use it to make a narrow hem on fabrics that ravel. Straight stitch ¼ inch (6 mm) from the raw edge of the hem, then press under the raw edge on the stitching. You can simply press under ¼ inch (6 mm) without doing the stitch, but the stitch helps when working with sheer fabrics. To complete the hem, press under another ¼ inch (6 mm) and stitch close to the upper fold.

APPLYING ELASTIC

Elastic can be stitched directly to the edge of lingerie or threaded through a casing (a tunnel of fabric).

stitched elastic

Use this method to apply lingerie elastic that has a decorative edge.

Make the elastic into a continuous loop by overlapping the ends and stitching them securely.

2

Use pins or a fabric marker to divide the elastic into equal parts, usually four parts for an armhole or a leg opening and eight parts for a larger waist edge. Divide and mark the lingerie edge the same way.

3

Pin the elastic right side down to the right side of the lingerie, matching the marks and aligning the straight edge of the elastic with the raw edge of the lingerie fabric.

4

Use a straight stitch to sew next to the decorative elastic edge, stretching the elastic flat to fit the lingerie and removing the pins as you go (figure 4).

Fold the elastic to the wrong side of the lingerie so the decorative elastic edge shows just beyond the folded edge of the lingerie. Use a short, narrow zigzag stitch to sew through all layers, stretching the elastic as you go (figure 5).

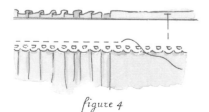

figure 4

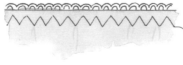

figure 5

cased elastic

Use this method to apply plain elastic to a waist edge.

Follow the project directions to fold under the raw edge of the lingerie fabric, and fold the casing. Press.

Edgestitch along the lower casing fold, leaving an opening in the stitching to insert the elastic.

Use a bodkin or safety pin (page 23) to insert the elastic in the casing (figure 6).

Overlap the elastic ends and stitch them securely.

Push the overlapped elastic ends into the casing. Stitch the casing opening closed.

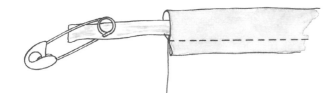

figure 6

NARROW STRAPS

Sometimes called spaghetti straps because they are as fine as a strand of pasta, skinny fabric straps are a favored lingerie detail. You can cut the fabric strips for the straps from matching or contrasting fabric.

folded and stitched

This method is easy, because there's no need to turn a narrow tube of fabric right side out.

1

To begin, cut a strip of fabric four times the desired finished width of the strap; for example, cut a 1-inch (2.5 cm) strip to make a ¼-inch (6 mm) strap.

2

Fold the long edges of the strip to the wrong side so the edges meet. Fold the edges once more so they align. Press and edgestitch.

stitched and turned

This method can produce very skinny straps and hides the stitching for a polished look.

1

To begin, cut a strip of fabric two times the desired finished width of the strap, plus ½ inch (1.3 cm) for two ¼-inch (6 mm) seam allowances; for example, cut a ¾-inch (1.9 cm) strip to make a ⅛-inch (3 mm) strap.

2

Fold the strip with right sides together, and stitch a ¼-inch (6 mm) seam.

Use a tube turner tool to turn the strap right side out (page 23). Or thread a blunt tapestry needle with all-purpose sewing thread, double the thread, and knot the ends. Sew a few stitches to anchor the thread at one end of the strap, work the needle eye-end first through the strap, and bring it out at the other end. Pull on the thread to turn the strap right side out. Clip the stitches to remove the needle and thread.

corded

Using a fine, soft filler cord, you can stitch a strap that uses the cord to turn the strap right side out as it fills with the cord.

1

To begin, cut a strip of fabric wide enough to wrap snugly around the cord, plus two seam allowances. Cut the cord two times the length of the strip plus 2 inches (5.1 cm).

2

Wrap the strip wrong side out around the cord, aligning the long raw edges of the strip and allowing about 1 inch (2.5 cm) of cord to extend beyond the strip at one end and the remaining cord to extend beyond the other end.

3

Attach a zipper foot on the sewing machine. Stitch close to the cord through both fabric layers. Stitch across the fabric layers and through the cord at one end of the strap. Pull the other end of the cord to turn the strap right side out as it fills with cord (figure 7). Trim the excess cord evenly with the ends of the strap.

figure 7

MAKING BIAS TAPE

Store-bought bias tape is handy, but when you're making an elegant dupioni silk suspender belt, you'll want matching bias tape made from the same silk fabric. Here's how to make your own.

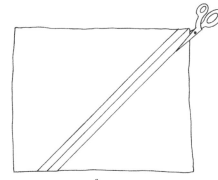

figure 8

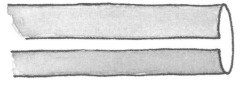

figure 9

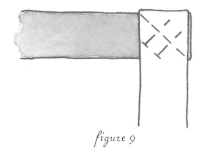

figure 10

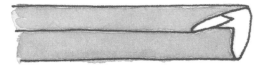

figure 11

Decide how wide you want the finished binding to be. Multiply that by four, and cut several strips that width on the bias (figure 8). For example, to make finished bias tape ¼ inch (6 mm) wide, cut bias strips 1 inch (2.5 cm) wide.

Stitch the strips end to end until you have one strip long enough to cover the raw edge you have in mind. For a professional look, and to reduce bulk, stitch the strips together on the diagonal (figure 9).

Fold and press the entire length of the strip right down the middle. Open up the strip and fold each of the sides in toward the pressed center (figure 10). Or, to make quick work of this step, use a bias tape maker (page 23).

Refold along the center line and press again (figure 11).

BUTTONHOLES

On lingerie, buttonholes are used most often to provide an opening for a drawstring. Use the buttonhole setting on a sewing machine or adjust the zigzag stitch setting to make a short, narrow stitch that aligns the stitches very closely together like a satin stitch.

Adding a layer of lightweight interfacing, behind the buttonhole on the wrong side, helps strengthen delicate fabrics and stabilize those that stretch. Sew a sample buttonhole on fabric scraps to check the machine settings and refine the length of the buttonhole so it provides an opening just a little larger than the drawstring. After stitching through the lingerie fabric and the interfacing, slit the buttonhole open with the tips of your scissors.

HOOK AND EYE CLOSURES

Occasionally you'll need to sew a hook and eye closure onto lingerie. Do this with some hand stitches.

1

To begin, thread a sewing needle with all-purpose thread, double the thread, and knot the ends.

2

Sew several stitches through each eyelet on the hook, and take a few stitches over the stem to hold the hook flat against the fabric. Secure the thread with a few small backstitches, and trim the thread ends.

3

In a similar way, sew several stitches through each eyelet on the eye.

EMBROIDERY

Only one of the projects actually calls for embroidery stitches (the garter on page 112), but don't let that stop you. A delicate line of embroidery stitches will add a personal touch to any lingerie item. Let your imagination be your guide. Here are a few stitches to get you started.

chain stitch

Also known as lazy daisy, this stitch can be worked in a circle to form a flower (figure 12).

french knot

This elegant little knot adds interest and texture when embroidering or embellishing (figure 13).

satin stitch

This stitch is composed of parallel rows of straight stitches, often used to fill in an outline (figure 14).

stem stitch

Also known as a crewel stitch, the stem stitch is often sewn to outline a shape (figure 15).

straight stitch

Use a simple straight stitch to create a motif (figure 16).

Got a craving to make your own lingerie now? Let your mind wander over the sweet little projects that follow.

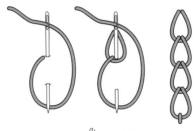

figure 12

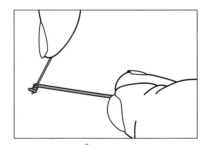

figure 13

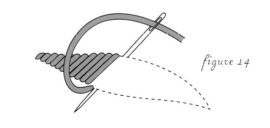

figure 14

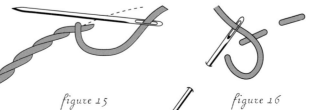

figure 15   figure 16

start your
day with
something
sweet

venus tanga

Let your inner goddess out with pretty little panties that fit like a glove. The secret is the stretchy lace—it contours to your body for the perfect fit, every time.

36

What You Do

1
Enlarge the template on page 121 and cut to your size. Cut out a crotch piece from the cotton jersey, and cut a second crotch piece at one end of the lace, next to the cut edge. Fold both ends of the remaining lace to meet in the middle. Place the template on one fold and use tailor's chalk to trace the angled line. Repeat on the other side, and cut out both body pieces.

2
With wrong sides facing, pin the crotch pieces. Using polyester thread, carefully serge them together around all the outer edges. Snip and carefully melt the ends of the threads with a lighter to keep them from unraveling.

3
With right sides facing, pin the two body pieces together at the angled ends. Serge the angled edges, snip the threads, and carefully melt the ends.

4
Turn the body right side out with the seams in the center. Lay the piece flat so that it resembles a V. With right sides facing, center the crotch along the seam, with the wide end at the point of the V. The point will stick out a little beyond the crotch. Run a zigzag stitch along the crotch edge. Be sure to backstitch to secure the stitching, and melt the thread ends. In the same way, attach the other end of the crotch to the other side of the panty. Trim the seam allowance where it extends beyond the crotch edges (figure 1).

5
Flip the panty right side out with the crotch at the bottom. Turn the crotch seam allowances up toward the panty and topstitch the seams flat with a three-step zigzag stitch, if available, or a regular zigzag stitch.

what you need

Sewing Kit (page 21)

Serger and sewing machine with a zigzag stitch

Small piece of cotton jersey to match the lace

1⅓ yards (1.2 m) of stretch lace, 6 or 7 inches (15.2 or 17.8 cm) wide

Polyester thread for serger and sewing machine

Lighter

Tiny ribbon rosette or bow

Sized for XS, S, M, L, XL

Seam allowance ¼ inch (6 mm)

6
Hand-sew a tiny rosette or bow within 1 inch (2.5 cm) from the top on the front center seam.

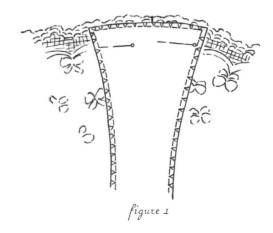

figure 1

sugarplum

Wrap yourself in a sensuous layer of silk and satin. Made of simple rectangles sized for a custom fit, this kimono is easy to make, but you'll find it terribly difficult to ever take off.

What You Do

1

On large rolls of paper, draw and label the pieces listed below. In each dimension, the first number is the width and the second is the length. Adjust these to fit your measurements, as needed, per the box on page 41.

- Back: 16 x 42 inches (40.6 cm x 106.7 cm)
- Front: 16 x 42 inches (40.6 cm x 106.7 cm)
- Sleeve: 19 x 15 (48.3 x 38.1 cm)
- Tie belt: 5 x 42 inches (12.7 cm x 106.7 cm)
- Sleeve borders: 5 x 19 inches (12.7 cm x 48.3 cm)
- Neck-front-hemline border: 5 x 50 inches (12.7 cm x 127 cm)

2

To draft the neckline, mark one long side of the kimono back as the fold. Measuring from that top corner, mark 1 inch (2.5 cm) down from the side and 3 inches (7.6 cm) across the top. Using these points as reference, draw a curved neckline (see figure 1 on page 41).

For the front V-neck, start at one corner and mark 3 inches (7.6 cm) along the top and 10 inches (25.4 cm) down the side. Draw a straight line between these points (see figure 1 on page 41).

3

To cut out the fabric, fold the chiffon fabric in half lengthwise, matching selvages. Cut one back on the fold, two fronts, and two sleeves. From the satin fabric, cut two tie belts, two sleeve borders, and four or five neck-front-hemline border pieces (the amount depends on the finished length of the kimono).

4

To make the body, with wrong sides facing, pin the fronts to the back at the shoulder seams and stitch with French seams (page 26).

what you need

Sewing Kit (page 21)

Ballpoint sewing machine needle (size 70/10 or 75/11)

Large sheets or rolls of paper

2⅞ yards (2.6 m) of sheer silk or synthetic chiffon, 44 inches (1.1 m) wide

1½ yards (1.4 m) of coordinating silk or synthetic satin, 44 inches (1.1 m) wide

Adjustable size (see Custom Sizing on page 41)

Seam allowance ½ inch (1.3 cm) unless otherwise noted

Sewing Lightweight Fabrics

Sheer, silky fabrics are lovely, but they can sometimes be tricky to sew. For best results, try some of these strategies:

- Shorten the length of the straight stitch slightly to prevent breakage.
- Use a smaller-size sewing machine needle.
- Use silk straight pins.
- When pressing, always use a press cloth.

5

To attach the sleeves, measure the top edge of each sleeve and mark the halfway point with a pin. Lay the body out flat, wrong side up, with the shoulder seam open in the middle. With wrong sides facing, line up the center of a top sleeve edge with the shoulder seam. Stitch with a French seam. Repeat on the other side.

6

To stitch the sides, with wrong sides facing, fold the kimono at the shoulder seams, lining up the sleeves on both sides. Stitch the back to the front at the side seam and underarm seam with a French seam, pivoting at the corner (figure 2).

7

To make the sleeve borders, with right sides facing, pin and stitch the ends of each sleeve band together, using a *regular* (not French) seam to make a continuous loop. With right sides facing, pin one side of each border to the end of a sleeve, matching underarm seams, and stitch. Trim the seam allowance and press it toward the band.

Fold under the opposite raw edge of the band ¼ inch (6 mm), then fold the band in half and pin the folded edge to the stitching line (figure 3). Topstitch through all layers.

8

To add the neckline-front-hemline border, measure and plan the locations of each joining seam in the border, preferably at the center back neckline, waistline, and side seams. For best results, pin a single band to the edge of the kimono, right sides facing, and stitch to within inches of a join area. Stop, break the stitching, and make the join in the exact location you wish. Attach this border in the same way as the sleeves border, mitering the front bottom corners of the kimono.

9

To make the tie belt, stitch the short ends together, right sides facing. Press the seams open. Fold the belt in half lengthwise and stitch all raw ends together, leaving an opening at the center large enough to turn. Turn the belt right side out and slip stitch the opening closed by hand.

Custom Sizing

If you follow the measurements provided in step 1, the completed kimono will be a generous medium size:

- It will fit someone with a 32- to 48-inch (81.3 to 121.9 cm) bust.
- The back length (from neck to hem) will measure 44 inches (111.8 cm).
- The finished sleeve length will be 31 inches (78.7 cm).

Measure your body to find the finished kimono size and lengths you desire. To shorten or lengthen the body or sleeves, simply add or subtract inches. To make the kimono wider or narrower, remember to divide the difference by 4 (to allow for two fronts and two backs), and adjust the front and back patterns by that amount.

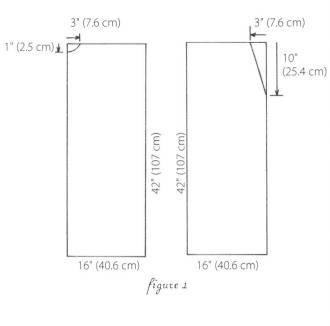

figure 1

figure 2

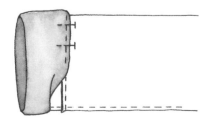

figure 3

Lemon drop

So sweet, so sunny! This little baby doll conjures up dreams of summer romance and sunrise strolls. The icing on the cake? A ruched bodice and satin spaghetti straps.

What You Do

1

Make paper patterns and label them, as follows:

- For the bodice front and back, cut out the pattern pieces.
- For the shirred front bodice overlay, measure and cut a paper rectangle 22 x 8 inches (55.9 x 20.3 cm).
- For the skirt, measure and cut a paper rectangle 50 x 25 inches (127 cm x 63.5 cm).
- For shoulder straps, measure and cut a paper pattern 1½ x 22 inches (3.8 x 55.9 cm).

To cut out the pieces, lay the tricot fabric flat and fold over one side, positioning the selvage near the center of the fabric. On the fold, cut two bodice fronts and two bodice backs. On the unfolded half of the fabric, cut one bodice overlay and one skirt. From the satin fabric, cut six shoulder straps on the bias.

2

Cut six pieces of filler cord, each 44 inches (111.8 cm) long, and use the satin fabric strips to make 6 straps (page 30). Trim the excess exposed cord at both ends, so each covered cord measures 18 inches (45.7 cm).

3

To gather the front bodice overlay, stitch long basting stitches ½ inch (1.3 cm) from the top and bottom edges, leaving long bobbin thread tails at each end. With wrong sides of both fabrics facing up, center a bodice front on top of the overlay, pinning at the side seams. Gather and pin the overlay to fit the bodice, evenly distributing the gathers (see figure 1 on page 45). Baste the fabrics together ¼ inch (6 mm) from all edges of the bodice. Trim the excess fabric from the overlay.

what you need

Sewing Kit (page 21)

Ballpoint sewing machine needle
(size 70/10 or 75/11)

Large sheets or rolls of paper

1 yard (0.9 m) of nylon tricot knit,
108 inches (2.7 m) wide, or 2 yards (1.8 m)
of lightweight knit, 60 inches (1.5 m) wide

⅝ yard (57.2 cm) of white polyester satin

8 yards (7.3 m) of filler cord,
³⁄₁₆ inch (5 mm) wide

1½ yards (1.4 m) of flat elastic,
¼ inch (6 mm) wide

1½ yards (1.4 m) of sheer ribbon,
1½ inches (3.8 cm) wide

Adjustable size
(see Custom Sizing on page 44)

Seam allowance ½ inch (1.3 cm)
unless otherwise noted

4

To attach the straps, with the gathered side of the bodice facing up, position three straps on the top curve of each bodice, about ¾ inch (1.9 cm) apart. Pin the cut ends even with the cut edge of the fabric. Stitch in place.

To sew the side seams, with right sides facing and cut edges even, pin and stitch together the side seams of the gathered bodice front to a back piece. Also stitch the side seams of the remaining bodice front and back, which will become the facing (figure 2). This is a good time to try on the bodice and determine the ideal length of the shoulder straps.

To assemble the bodice, with right sides facing and side seams aligned, pin together the upper edges of the bodice. Bring the loose strap ends between the back bodice and the facing, and position them directly across from the strap fronts, about ¾ inch (1.9 cm) apart, at the length desired. Stitch the upper edge of the bodice, catching the straps as you sew (figure 3). Turn the assembly right side out. Understitch the upper edge of the bodice close to the seam, through the facing and all seam allowances but not through the bodice. Pin together the lower edge of the bodice to the facing and baste.

Custom Sizing

To adjust the pattern size, measure around your bust. The circumference of the bodice shown is 37 inches (93.9 cm). To make the pattern wider or narrower, remember to divide the difference by 4 and adjust both front and back by that amount.

The bodice is sized for a B cup. For a C or D cup bust, reshape the fullness of the bodice at the top and bottom edges of the pattern front.

Right Side vs. Wrong Side

When examined closely, the right side of a knit fabric (which looks similar to a T-shirt) shows a small version of a knit stitch with vertical V shapes. The wrong side shows a more horizontal wavy stitch similar to a purl stitch.

Sewing Knit Fabrics

For best results when sewing knit fabrics, try some of these strategies:

- Shorten the length of your straight stitch to 10 stitches per inch (2.5 cm), or 2.0 mm.
- Change the machine needle to a ballpoint or stretch needle.
- Use ballpoint or silk straight pins.
- For nylon tricot, also consider using a lightweight polyester or lingerie thread.

7

To make the skirt, with right sides facing, stitch the center back seam of the skirt. Finish the seams (see box below). Stitch long basting stitches ⅜ inch (1 cm) from the top edge, leaving long bobbin thread tails at each end. With right sides facing, pin the upper edge of the skirt to the lower edge of the bodice, matching the center back seams and distributing fullness evenly. Stitch together with a ⅝-inch (1.6 cm) seam allowance. Trim all seam allowances except for the bodice facing allowance. Pin this seam allowance flat against the top of the skirt and stitch a ⅜-inch (1 cm) casing, leaving an opening to insert the elastic. Thread the elastic through the casing and adjust to fit.

8

Determine the skirt length and hem. For a fancy finish, use a hem stitch, topstitching close to the fold and allowing the zigzag to fall off the fold. This creates a scalloped look to the folded edge. A second row of straight stitches ¼ inch (6 mm) from the hem stitch will help hold the hem flat. Trim the excess fabric close to the stitching (figure 4).

9

Snip a V in the ends of the sheer ribbon. Tie a neat bow and hand-sew in place at the bottom center of the bodice.

Finishing the Seams

Clean-finish the seam allowance through both layers of fabric with a three-step zigzag stitch close to the seam. To prevent tunneling, avoid a one-step zigzag. Trim the seam allowance close to the seam finish and press the seam to one side.

figure 1

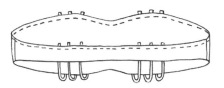

figure 2

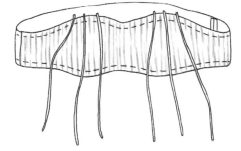

figure 3

figure 4

This playful chemise is so adorable you'll be tempted to wear it outdoors as a sundress. And why not? The fanciful patchwork border deserves to be shown off.

What You Do

1

Cut out the pattern pieces. Cut out the front and back from the white fabric. Cut the bra from the solid color, marking the dart lines and center front.

2

Stitch the dart on the wrong side of both bra pieces. On the sides without a dart, press under ¼ inch (6 mm). Pin rickrack over the folded edges, on the wrong side of the bra, with the wavy edge of rickrack showing on the right side. From the right side, topstitch close to the edge.

3

To make the bra straps, cut two 20-inch (50.8 cm) strips from the binding tape. (This should be more than you need, and you can adjust the length later.) Stitch the long open edge of each binding strip. On the right side of each bra piece, at the top, stitch a strap in place. Press the seam allowance toward the bra and topstitch.

4

With right sides facing, pin the bra to the camisole front, crossing over 1 inch (2.5 cm) at the center of the front (see figure 1 on page 48). Stitch, and press the seam allowance toward the body.

5

From the solid and print fabric strips, cut out 44 to 52 triangles for the patchwork (the exact number you need will vary, depending on your size). Lay out the triangles in four long bands (two for the front and two for the back), mixing colors and fabrics as you like. Stitch the triangles together (see figure 2 on page 48). Lay the strips next to the bottom of the camisole to see whether they're long enough; add more triangles to each strip if necessary.

what you need

Sewing Kit (page 21)

1 yard (0.9 m) of white cotton fabric

¼ yard (22.9 cm) of cotton fabric in a solid color, for the bra

1 yard (0.9 m) of rickrack

3 yards (2.7 m) of bias binding tape

8 strips of cotton fabrics in solid colors, cut 5 inches (12.7 cm) wide x the width of the fabric

4 strips of gingham and flower prints, cut 5 inches (12.7 cm) wide x the width of the fabric

Sized for M, L, XL

Seam allowance ¼ inch (6 mm)

6

With right sides facing, pin two strips together, lining up the triangle bases and points (this doesn't need to be exact). Stitch along one long side, and press the seams open. Do the same with the remaining two strips. Fold each pair of strips in half, lay the patchwork template on the fold, and trim to shape. With right sides facing, stitch one patchwork band to the front and one to the back.

7

Make a narrow hem at the top edge of the back by pressing under ¼ inch (6 mm), and another ¼ inch (6 mm). Edgestitch in place. With right sides together, and the patchwork strips aligned, stitch the front to the back at the side seams.

8

Finish the bottom edge with binding tape. Attach the straps at the back to fit.

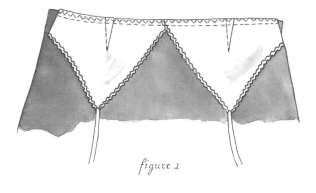

figure 1

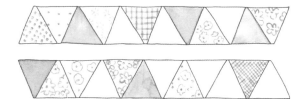

figure 2

You hit the snooze button more than once, and like to drink cups of tea in bed. The cheery fabric used in these lounging separates is actually a vintage sheet—making you feel like a dream girl.

hello, yellow

49

what you need

Sewing Kit (page 21)

1 vintage flat sheet, single/twin size, generally 66 x 96 inches (1.7 x 2.4 m)

1 small piece of fusible interfacing for reinforcing buttonholes

1 yard (0.9 m) of single-fold bias binding tape in a matching color, ½ inch (1.3 cm) wide

2⅜ yards (2.2 m) of ribbon in a matching color, ⅜ inch (1 cm) wide

1 yard (0.9 m) of soft elastic, ½ inch (1.3 cm) wide

Sized for M, L, XL

Seam allowance ⅜ inch (1 cm)

What You Do

1

Cut out the pattern pieces. With right sides facing, fold the sheet in half lengthwise and lay out all five pattern pieces for the nightie and shorts. Cut out the nightie pieces, marking the fold lines, dots, buttonhole positions, and A and B ends of the sleeve. Decide how long you want the shorts to be, adding 1¼ inches (3.2 cm) for the hem, and cut out the pieces.

NIGHTIE TOP

1

On the fronts, press a small patch of fusible interfacing to the back of the buttonholes where marked. Stitch a buttonhole on both fronts.

2

With right sides facing, stitch the front pieces together at the center seam. Starting at the top, stitch from the edge to the dot, pivot, and stitch to the bottom edge. Notch the seam at the dot (figure 1). Press the seams open.

3

With right sides facing, stitch the back pieces together at the center seam. Press the seams open.

4

With right sides facing, stitch the front to the back, at the side seams, and press the seams open.

5

On the bottom of each sleeve edge (opposite the fold line edge), make a hem by pressing under ¼ inch (6 mm), then another ¼ inch (6 mm). Stitch in place. With right sides facing, pin the sleeve to the nightie, matching sleeve dots at A and B to the front and back of the nightie. Baste the ends of both sleeves by stitching from the dot to the opposite edge of the sleeve (figure 2).

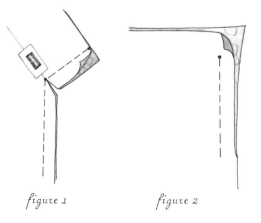

figure 1   figure 2

6

To finish the armhole seams, press one side of the binding tape flat. With right sides facing (and overlapping the wrong side of the sleeve), start at the dot and pin the pressed side of the binding to the armhole edge on each side. Stitch in place (figure 3). Remove the basting thread, then trim the seam allowance and clip the curved edges. Press the binding to the wrong side of the fabric. Move the sleeve out of the way and edgestitch the binding (figure 4).

7

Where the casings overlap above the dot, on the right side of the front and back, turn under the raw edge and stitch. Press under the top edge of the casing ¼ inch (6 mm), then press another ⅞ inch (2.2 cm), more or less, with the buttonholes landing on the fold. Edgestitch the casing in place.

8

Using a safety pin, feed the ribbon through the casing, in one buttonhole and out the other. Gather to fit and tie with a bow.

9

Check the length of the garment. To make the hem, press under ¼ inch (6 mm), then press under 1 inch (2.5 cm). Edgestitch in place.

SHORTS

1

With right sides facing, line up and pin the inner leg seams of each front/back piece (figure 5). Stitch the seam, and finish the raw edges using a zigzag or an overlock stitch.

2

Turn one leg right side out and place it inside the other leg with right sides facing. Pin the crotch seam. Stitch from the front to the back (figure 6). Trim the seam allowance and clip the curved edges. Reinforce the seam with an overlock stitch and press the seam allowance to one side.

3

To form a casing, press under the top raw edge of the shorts ¼ inch (6 mm), then press under 1 inch (2.5 cm). Edgestitch around the entire casing, leaving a small opening at the back. Feed the elastic through the casing and pin the elastic to itself. Try on the shorts for fit and adjust the elastic. Cut to the right length if necessary, overlap the ends, and stitch the elastic. Stitch to close the casing opening.

4

Hem by pressing under the bottom edge ¼ inch (6 mm), then pressing under 1 inch (2.5 cm). Stitch.

figure 3   figure 4

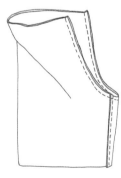

figure 5   figure 6

beaded bliss

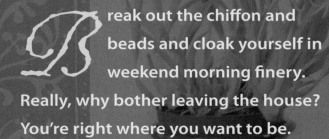

Break out the chiffon and beads and cloak yourself in weekend morning finery. Really, why bother leaving the house? You're right where you want to be.

What You Do

1

Cut out the pattern pieces. On the fronts, press a small patch of fusible interfacing to the back of the buttonholes where marked. Stitch a buttonhole on both fronts.

2

Fuse the interfacing to the wrong side of the facings, following the manufacturer's instructions.

3

With right sides facing, pin the front and back together at the shoulders. Double stitch the seams (see the box on page 54) and press to one side.

4

With right sides facing, stitch the front and back facings together at the sides. Finish the raw edges by pressing them under ¼ inch (6 mm) and stitching all the way around (see figure 1 on page 54).

5

With right sides facing, pin the facing to the front and back, matching the shoulder seams. Baste down the center front from the raw edge to the dot. Stitch the seams on either side of the basting line, taking one stitch across the dot at the bottom. Cut down the center basted line to above the small dot (see figure 2 on page 54).

6

Complete the neckline by stitching all the way around the edge, restitching 1 inch (2.5 cm) down the front edges on both sides. Trim the seam allowances.

what you need

Sewing Kit (page 21)

3⅜ yards (3.1 m) of chiffon

⅜ yard (34.3 cm) of fusible interfacing

2¾ yards (2.5 m) of beaded trim,
½ inch (1.3 cm) wide

Sized for XS/S, S/M, M/L

⅝ inch (1.6 cm)

designer ● **JOAN K. MORRIS**

53

7

Turn the facing right side out and press. Tack the facing down by hand at the shoulder seams. Topstitch ¼ inch (6 mm) from the edge around the neck and the center V (see figure 3 on page 54).

8

With right sides facing, pin each sleeve to an armhole edge, lining up the shoulder dot with the shoulder seams. Double stitch the seams and press the seam allowances toward the sleeve (figure 4).

9

With right sides facing, pin the underarm edges of the sleeve, and the tunic front and back together, matching seams and raw edges. Leave the seam open below the circle on the side seam (figure 5). Double stitch the seams and press.

10

Hem the bottom of the sleeves by pressing under ¼ inch (6 mm), then pressing under another ¼ inch (6 mm). Stitch and press. Do the same along the front and back bottom edges. Hem the side seams last, stitching across both seams above the slit (figure 6).

11

To apply the beaded trim, start in the center back of the neck. Fold under the edge of the beaded strip and hand-sew it in place ¼ inch (6 mm) from the edge of the neckline. When the

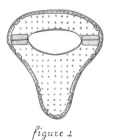

figure 1

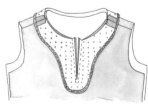

figure 2

Working with Chiffon

Sheer, slippery fabrics like chiffon can be tricky to work with. Here are a couple of pointers:

- Before cutting out pattern pieces, place a large piece of felt or wool fabric on the cutting surface. Lay the chiffon on top of the felt. Pin the pattern pieces in place through both fabric layers. When cutting, cut on top of the wool and through the chiffon.

- To finish the seams, use a double-stitched seam: Sew the ⅝-inch (1.6 cm) seam first, and then stitch again ⅛ inch (3 mm) away, toward the raw edge. Trim the raw edges close to the second row of stitches.

two ends meet, cut off the trim with enough left to fold under and meet the beginning. Do the same around the bottom of the sleeves.

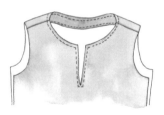

figure 3

figure 4

figure 5

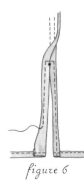

figure 6

beaded bliss

You're a natural temptress, and a bit of a chameleon, and you aren't afraid to try something new. You love the idea of reinventing your wardrobe, starting with this peachy slip-turned-bra.

EVE

what you need

Sewing Kit (page 21)

1 vintage slip

Stretch lace, 2½ inches (6.4 cm) wide
x long enough to encircle your torso

Commercial fabric dye and
dyeing supplies (page 15)

Sizes vary

Seam allowance ¼ inch (6 mm)

What You Do

1

Try on the slip. With pins or fabric marker, mark under your bust where the bottom of the bra will be. Take off the slip and cut 1 inch (2.5 cm) below your marked bust line. Cut off the back at the side seams and detach the straps from the back, keeping them connected in the front.

2

Wrap the stretch lace around your ribs below your bust, with the ends in front at the middle of your chest. With right sides facing, pin the ends together at a comfortable tightness and expand your ribs by breathing deeply, to test the fit. Mark the top edge of the lace.

figure 1

Treasure Hunt

Look for a vintage slip—one with lace around the bust and adjustable straps— in Grandma's closet, at rummage sales, or in thrift shops. Slips that are 100 percent polyester won't hold dye, so look for one with rayon or cotton in it. A polyester blend will only partially absorb the dye, so it will be a lighter shade. Another idea: Instead of buying stretch lace, you could recycle the lace waistband on a favorite pair of panties.

3

Using a ruler that shows a 60° angle, trace and cut the lace at that angle, with the longest point at the top edge of the lace. Stitch the seam and finish the edge with a narrow zigzag stitch (or use a serger) (figure 1).

4

Try on the stretch lace and the cut slip top. Position the angled seam in the center front of the top. Tuck the edge of the bra behind the lace (next to your skin) and pin. In the same way, pin the sides of the top to the lace, where you'd like it to be, then carefully tuck and pin the rest of the top to the lace for the best fit. You may need to make darts or gathers. Experiment to find where you want the straps to attach in the back, and pin them in place.

5

Carefully remove the bra. Starting on one side, topstitch the top to the lace, using a slight zigzag stitch. In the same way, stitch each strap to the back, folding under the ends for neatness.

6

Dye the fabric according to the manufacturer's instructions (see also page 15).

oilies aren't just for sitting under a bonbon bowl. Dish up a new brand of sweetness with some pretty crochet, delicate lace, and soft jersey cotton. This gives a whole new meaning to eye candy.

pretty swirl

what you need

Sewing Kit (page 21)

1 crocheted table doily—sizes will vary; the
one shown was 16 inches (40.6 cm) across

⅓ yard (61 cm) of thin,
flesh-colored jersey fabric

3 x 24-inch (7.6 x 61 cm) piece of
stretch cotton fabric for the torso strap

24 inches (61 cm) of ribbon,
¼ inch (6 mm) wide for the lacing

30 inches (76.2 cm) of lace,
1 inch (2.5 cm) wide for the shoulder straps

Bra hook closure for the torso strap
(could be recycled from an old bra)

Adjustable size

Seam allowance ¼ inch (6 mm)

Sizing the Bra

The project template is for a medium-size bra. If
you'd like to alter the size of the bra, take a look
at the under-bust size, cup size, and
strap length.

Under-Bust Size While wearing a bra, line up a
measuring tape with the bottom of the bra, and
measure all the way around your torso. Our bra
is sized to fit a 30- to 32-inch (76.2 to 81.3 cm)
under-bust size. If you are larger or smaller than
that, add or subtract inches as needed.

Cup Size Add or subtract inches from the template as needed.

Strap Length For a comfy fit, it's important
that the straps be the right length. Measure
from the bust apex to your mid-shoulder front,
then multiply that figure by two, and add 1 inch
(2.5 cm) for seam allowance.

What You Do

1

Enlarge the template on page 123. Use it as a guide to cut a
trapezoid from the doily. Flip the template over and cut an
identical trapezoid that is a mirror image of the first one. Cut
two trapezoids from the jersey fabric in the same way.

2

With right sides facing, pin a doily piece to a fabric piece, and
stitch around the entire perimeter, leaving a small opening for
turning. Turn right side out and hand-sew the opening shut.
Press flat. Do the same with the remaining pieces. Set aside.

To make the torso straps: Lay the 24-inch (61 cm) strip of cotton fabric flat, and turn under both sides along its length, about ¾ inch (1.9 cm), so they overlap. Stitch them together by running a zigzag stitch down the middle of the strip (figure 1). Because this kind of fabric doesn't ravel, there is no need to finish the raw edges. Cut the strip in half, to make two straps 12 inches (30.5 cm) long.

To attach the torso straps, lay one of the doily-jersey pieces right side down. On the wrong side, fold the bottom edge up about 1 inch (2.5 cm) on the diagonal, as marked on the template. At the narrow end, tuck in the end of one of the jersey straps and pin. Hand-sew the folded edge (so the stitches won't show in the front) (figure 2) and machine-stitch the strap flat at the outer edge, using a zigzag stitch.

To lace the two bra cups together, attach a pin to one end of the ¼-inch (6 mm) ribbon or wrap the end in masking tape. Thread the lace through an existing crochet hole at the top of one side of the bra, then thread it through an existing hole at the top of the other side. Weave back and forth between the two, down to the bottom and back up again, as though you were lacing a shoe. Tie the lace in a bow at the top.

Try on the bra and adjust the length of the torso strap. Trim off what you don't need and hand-sew or machine-stitch the bra hook closure to the ends of the straps.

To make the shoulder straps, cut the 1-inch (2.5 cm) lace in half. Stitch each one to the top corner of a bra cup. Again try on the bra, to measure how long these straps need to be. Add 1 inch (2.5 cm) to the measurement and fold under the ends of each strap by that amount; stitch in place to make a small loop. Thread the cotton strip through the loop on each side (figure 3).

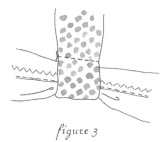

figure 1

figure 2

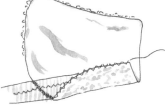

figure 3

afternoon indulgences

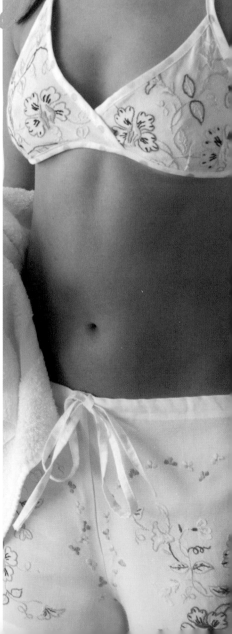

while away
the day in
something tasty

amelie

A hopeless romantic, that's you—dreaming of Paris, jotting poems in your journal, and gazing at strangers. This charming set was made with you in mind, using vintage table lace and a darling striped print.

What You Do

PANTIES

1

To make the templates, lay the panties or bikini bottom flat and trace first the front, then the back, on two separate pieces of paper. Add ½ inch (1.3 cm) outside the seamline, all the way around both panty outlines, for seam allowance. Cut out both templates. Measure the width of the back piece crotch seam. Cut a template that is the same width x 4½ inches (11.4 cm) long.

2

Pin the front and back templates onto the stretch fabric, paying attention to the orientation of your fabric. If you are using stripes, have them run vertically down the panties. Cut out both pieces. Cut out the crotch template with the stripes running horizontally across the fabric.

3

Place the fabric pieces as shown in figure 1 on page 65. With right sides facing, stitch the ends of the crotch to the bottoms of both front and back.

4

From the scrap cotton fabric, cut a 5½ x 3½-inch (14 x 8.9 cm) rectangle. Press under the two short ends of the fabric. With wrong sides facing, pin this piece to the crotch of the panties, covering the seams on both ends. Edgestitch the folded ends in place. Fold the sides of the striped fabric over the white cotton, and pin and stitch in place (figure 2, page 65). You will continue this seam in step 6.

5

With right sides facing, stitch the panties front to the back, at the sides. Try the panties on for fit, and adjust as needed.

(continued on next page)

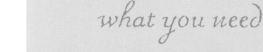

what you need

Sewing Kit (page 21)

Panties or bikini bottom that fits you nicely

⅔ yard (61 cm) of sturdy cotton stretch fabric

Scrap piece of white 100% cotton
stretch fabric (for crotch lining)

2 vintage linen table doilies—sizes will vary;
those shown were 11½ inches (29.2 cm) across

2 hook and eye clasps (new or recycled)

40 inches (1 m) of sturdy,
lace ribbon (for bra straps)

●

Adjustable Size

Seam allowance ½ inch (1.3 cm)

63

Sizing the Bra

The project template is for a medium-size bra. The stretch fabric and the adjustable bra closure in back allow for size flexibility. However, if you'd like to alter the size of the bra, take a look at the under-bust size, cup size, and strap length.

Under-Bust Size While wearing a bra, line up a measuring tape with the bottom of the bra, and measure all the way around your torso. Our bra is sized for a 30- to 32-inch (76.2 to 81.3 cm) under-bust size. If you're larger or smaller than that, add or subtract inches as needed.

Cup Size Doilies vary in size, and you'll want one to fit your bust line. Measure from the center of the under-bust of one breast up to 1 inch (2.5) above the apex of the bust (or wherever you'd like the bra to reach). The radius of the doily (from the center to the outer edge) should match your measurement (no seam allowance needed). After adjusting the cup size, adjust the length of the 14-inch (35.6 cm) fabric strip for the hem, as needed.

Strap Length For a comfy fit, it's important that the straps be the right length. Measure from the bust apex to your mid-shoulder front, then multiply that figure by two, and add 1 inch (2.5 cm) for seam allowance.

Tracing Tip

One way to trace the panty outline is to smooth it out flat, front side up, and lay a piece of scrap paper on top. Use the side of a crayon without a paper wrapping to carefully rub on the paper. The crayon will pick up the lines from the seams of the panties. With a second piece of paper, repeat this process for the back.

amelie

Hem all sides of the panties, using a tiny zigzag stitch. Depending on the fabric, you may need to cut small slits into the seam of the fabric where it is convex, or cut small triangles where the fabric is concave, to make a smooth hemline.

Cut out the "lace" around the perimeter of one of the doilies, ½ inch (1.3 cm) from where the lace begins (figure 3, page 65). Turn the panties right side out and pin the lacy piece to the top front hemmed edge of the panties. You can turn one edge for neatness, or leave it raw and let it ravel a bit. Stitch in place, using a small zigzag stitch. The curve of the piece will form a naturally ruffled edge to the lace.

BRA

To make the cups, fold one doily in half, and cut on the fold line. Fold one doily half again to make a quarter piece. On the cut edge, pin or make a mark 1 inch (2.5 cm) from the fold. Stitch a tapered line from there to the opposite end of the fold, making a dart (figure 4). Open the doily and press. Repeat with the other doily half.

With the stripes running vertically, cut a rectangle of fabric 11 inches (27.9 cm) wide x 30 inches (76.2 cm) or your underbust measurement (see the Sizing the Bra box on page 64). This will be the body of the bra. Fold the fabric in half along its length, and press the crease. Now fold the fabric in half in the other direction, along the width, but don't press.

Place one doily half along the center fold, and mark with a pin on the striped fabric where the center of the doily hits (figure 5). Remove the doily and unfold at the center. Measure about ¾ inch (1.9 cm) to either side of the pin and make a dart through two layers of fabric (figure 6). Refold the fabric at the center and repeat the process on the opposite side.

Pin the first doily where it was originally, lining up the darts. Stitch the doily around the curved edge, through the folded fabric, leaving the top cut edge unstitched. Repeat for the other doily on the opposite side.

figure 1

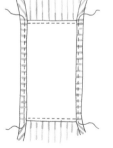

figure 2

figure 3

figure 4

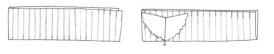

figure 5

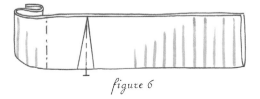

figure 6

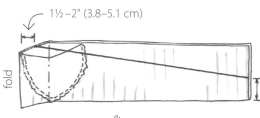

5

Refold the rectangle in the center as before. From the top of the fold, measure 1½ to 2 inches (3.8 to 5.1 cm) along the edge and mark the spot with a pin. On the far (raw) end, measure 1½ inches (3.8 cm) up from the bottom edge and mark with a pin. Using the straight edge, draw a line on the fabric from one pin to the other (figure 7). **Note:** The exact location of the first point will vary depending on how you've customized the bra size, so experiment with what feels right. When you're satisfied, unfold the fabric at the center and cut along the diagonal line through both layers of fabric. Refold and use the first side as a template for cutting the other side to match.

6

To make the curved top of the bra, cut a soft, arched line through one cup to the folded edge (figure 8). Match this cut on the other side.

1½–2" (3.8–5.1 cm)

fold

figure 7

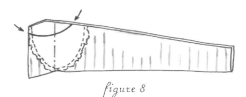

figure 8

7

Cut out the fabric beneath the doily halves, leaving ½ inch (1.3 cm) of fabric intact along the bottom, for strength. From the striped fabric, cut a strip about 1¼ x 14 inches (3.2 x 35.6 cm). Use it as binding to enclose the top raw edge of the bra, folding it over as necessary to wrap around the curves (figure 9). **Note:** The stretch fabric we used doesn't ravel, so there is no need to fold over the raw edges. Fold over and stitch the raw edge of the doily, as needed. Run a straight stitch along the entire bottom of the bra. Leave the ends of the bra open.

8

Cut the lace ribbon into two pieces, each 20 inches (50.8 cm) long. Turn under one end and pin to the outer top edge of one doily cup. Repeat with the other ribbon on the other side. Try on the bra and decide how long the straps need to be, and where you want to attach them to the back. Fold under the ends and stitch in place. Secure the hook and eye clasps in place (see page 33).

figure 9

Want to start a rumor? Make these bloomers! Sheer cotton voile fabric turns you into the talk of the town—or at least the neighborhood, if you wear them out to fetch the paper.

What You Do

1

Cut out the pattern pieces, and cut out the front, back, and flounce from the cotton voile.

2

With right sides facing, pin the top edge of each flounce to the bottom edge of a front/back piece. Stitch in place.

3

With right sides facing, line up and pin the inner leg seams of each front/back piece (figure 1). Stitch the seam, then finish the raw edges using a zigzag or an overlock stitch. Press the seam in the direction of the flounce.

4

Hem the flounce on your sewing machine, or roll and sew by hand. Press.

5

Turn one leg right side out and place it inside the other leg with right sides facing. Pin the crotch seam. Stitch from front to back (figure 2). Trim the seam allowance and clip the curved edges. Reinforce the seam with an overlock stitch and press the seam allowance to one side.

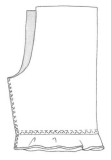

figure 1

figure 2

what you need

Sewing Kit (page 21)

Hemming foot for sewing machine (optional)

1½ yards (1.4 m) of
lightweight printed cotton voile

Scrap of fusible interfacing
to reinforce buttonholes

1⅔ yards (1.5 m) of satin
ribbon, ½ inch (1.3 cm) wide

Sized for M, L, XL

Seam allowance ⅜ inch (1 cm)

designer ● **FIONA HESFORD**

To form a casing, press under the top raw edge of the bloomers ¼ inch (6 mm), then press under again 1 inch (2.5 cm). On the front, draw two vertical lines for buttonholes, positioned 1 inch (2.5 cm) from the center seam on both sides. Open up the casing and fuse a small piece of fusible interfacing behind both buttonhole lines. Make both buttonholes.

Pin the casing down and stitch close to the edge. Press. Feed the ribbon through the casing, in one buttonhole and out the other. Gather to fit and tie with a bow.

skirt flirt

This luscious slip skirt is to dye for. Pick your favorite colors to transform some plain slips, and cut a fashionable sash from a vintage bed sheet. It's easy, and oh-so dreamy.

what you need

Sewing Kit (page 21)

2 vintage slips

1 vintage bed sheet

Commercial fabric dye in coordinating colors
and dyeing supplies (page 15, optional)

●

Sizes vary

Seam allowance ½ inch (1.3 cm)

What You Do

1

Decide how long you want your wrap skirt to be; it will be reversable. Lay one slip on top of the other, aligned at the bottom. Measure from the bottom to your desired length, add ½ inch (1.3 cm) for seam allowance, and cut off the slip tops. Keep the tops for making bras (page 55).

2

Cut each slip open at a side seam. Depending on the size of the slips, the open width may or may not match, which is fine. Check the raw edges, where you cut the slip. Most slip fabrics won't fray, but if your fabric is an exception, turn the sides under ¼ inch (6 mm) twice, and stitch. Don't bother with the top edge, beause it will be enclosed in the waistband. Set the slips aside.

3

Cut from one corner to the opposite corner of the sheet to make a 4½-inch-wide (11.4 cm) strip of bias fabric. This will become your waistband strap. Make sure that this is long enough to wrap around your waist or hips twice. If you do not have enough of one length, cut a second bias strip and stitch the two together at one end.

4

Dye the slips and the bias strip, following the manufacturer's instructions (see also page 15). You can dye them all the same color or different colors. For a mottled or tie-dye effect, tie knots in the fabrics or bunch up different sections with rubber bands.

5

When the fabrics are dry, lay the slips flat on a smooth surface, wrong sides facing, with tops and bottoms aligned. Shift one slip to the left and the other to the right, until half of one slip overlaps half of the other slip, with equal amounts of each slip on the sides. Pin the overlapped layers together along the top edge and baste. Mark the center of the top edge (which will be the center of the overlapped section) with a pin.

skirt flirt

Treasure Hunt

Hunt through a favorite thrift store for vintage slips. Pure polyester won't hold dye, so check the fiber content for a slip blended with rayon or cotton.

To make the waistband strap, press the bias strip in half along its length, wrong sides facing. Open up the strip and press the sides 1 inch (2.5 cm) toward the center, and refold. The folded strap will be about 1¼ inches (3.2 cm) wide.

Find the center of the strap and match it up with the center of the slip's top edge. There should be an equal amount of strap on both sides of the slips. Enclose the entire top edge with the bias strip, pinning as you go. Tuck in the raw edges at the ends of the straps to make a flat or diagonal end. Stitch from one end of the strap to the other, using a straight or zigzag stitch.

With the overlapped slips in front, put on the skirt and wrap it around to tie in the front. You can stop here, or you can make a buttonhole in the strap for a tidier waistband. Put one hand on your hip and mark that side of the waistband. It will likely be about where the slips start to overlap. Make either a vertical or a horizontal buttonhole at that spot.

calla lily

This embroidered
sleep set serves up
just the right touch
of pretty and feminine. Would
you believe it's made from a vintage tablecloth? Only this time,
you get to be the centerpiece.

74

What You Do

1

Cut out the pattern pieces. From the spotted fabric, cut out the back yokes. On the bias, cut about 3 yards (2.7 m) of 1½-inch (3.8 cm) strips for bias binding. Cut two more strips, each about 26 inches (66 cm) long, for the shorts drawstring.

2

Position the remaining templates on the tablecloth for the best use of the embroidered sections, placing the two bra pieces and the shorts front pieces in the four embroidered corners, if possible. Cut out the pieces, marking the buttonhole positions on the shorts front.

BRA

1

Make the strips into bias binding (page 32).

2

Stitch the dart on the wrong side of both bra pieces. Enclose the inside raw edges of the bra triangle with bias binding and stitch. Trim the binding to the correct length (see figure 1 on page 76). Overlap the inside edges of the bra by about 2 inches (5.1 cm); pin, check for fit against your body, and baste.

3

Cut two pieces of binding tape 22 inches (55.9 cm) long. Line up one end of each binding strip with the bottom outer edges of the bra. Enclose the outside raw edges of the bra triangle and stitch from the bottom to the top. Continue stitching the edges of the binding together to make neck straps at the top of the triangle.

what you need

Sewing Kit (page 21)

1 vintage embroidered tablecloth, preferably with embroidery in each of the four corners

1 yard (0.9 m) of spotted cotton fabric to coordinate with tablecloth

Bias tape maker for single-fold binding tape that is ¾ inch (1.9 cm) wide (optional)

½ yard (45.7 cm) of elastic, ⅜ inch (1 cm) wide

•

Sized for S, M, L

Seam allowance ⅝ inch

Cut a piece of binding tape about 54 inches (1.4 m) long. Fold it in half and mark its center. Unfold the tape and position the center mark in the center of the bra front. Enclose the raw edges, and stitch the binding to the lower edge of the bra. Continue stitching the edges of the binding together to make the side straps.

Put on the bra and tie the side straps in the back. To determine the correct length for the neck straps, have a friend help you mark where they need to intersect the back straps. Stitch the ends of the neck straps into loops, to the correct length. Feed the back straps through the loops (figure 2).

SHORTS

With right sides facing, stitch each back yoke to a back bottom. Press the seams up toward the yoke and topstitch in place.

With right sides together, join each front piece to a back piece at the side seams.

With right sides facing, line up and pin the inner leg seams of each front/back piece (figure 3). Stitch the seam, then finish the raw edges using a zigzag or an overlock stitch.

Turn one leg right side out and place it inside the other leg with right sides facing. Pin the crotch seam. Stitch from front to back (figure 4). Trim the seam allowance and clip the curved edges. Reinforce the seam with an overlock stitch and press the seam allowance to one side.

For the casing, make two buttonholes on either side of the center front seam, as indicated on the template. Press under the top edge ¼ inch (6 mm), then another ¾ inch (1.9 cm). Edgestitch the casing along the back only. Measure your waist and divide that number in half. Cut a strip of elastic to that length. Thread the elastic through the back casing and stitch one end to a side seam. Gather the casing in the back, adjust the length of the elastic for fit, if necessary, and stitch the other end of the elastic to the opposite side seam.

To make the drawstring, stitch the two 26-inch (66 cm) lengths of binding closed on the long folded side and both ends. At each side seam, inside the casing (aligned with the end of the elastic), stitch one end of a drawstring. Thread the end of the drawstring through the nearest buttonhole, and stitch the casing closed, taking care not to stitch the edge of the drawstring.

To hem, press under the bottom edge ¼ inch (6 mm), then press under another ¾ inch (1.9 cm) and stitch.

figure 1   figure 2

figure 3   figure 4

scarlet

This little slip dress has places to go! Find two vintage slips, dye them the colors you desire, add lace, decorative ribbon, and a cool screen print, and *va va voom*! It's a look that works both in and out of the bedroom.

What You Do

1

Wash the slips to remove any oils or residue and to ensure even dyeing. Dye them different coordinating colors, following the manufacturer's instructions (also see page 15). Allow them to dry completely.

2

Pin the wide lace at the bottom of the slip, directly behind the hem or any existing lace. Overlap the ends by about ½ inch (1.3 cm). Stitch the lace to the hem by hand, or use a sewing machine (you can leave the ends raw; they won't ravel). You can hide your stitches with careful placement and matching thread, or use brightly colored thread and decorative stitches to have the stitching become a part of the slip.

3

You can replace the straps on one or both slips with ribbon. Carefully remove one strap, detaching it completely from the back and leaving the front tab in place (the short loop of fabric with a metal ring that holds the rest of the strap). Save the hardware from the removed strap (if it's broken or not reusable, new strap hardware can be purchased at a fabric store). Leave the second strap in place for now, and refer to it for reassembly of the first strap.

4

Fold under the end of the ribbon once and stitch it to prevent raveling. By hand or with a machine, stitch the ribbon to the back of the slip in the same place where the old strap was removed. Thread the new ribbon back through the strap hardware in the same way as the old strap (figure 1). Fold the end under and stitch, which will keep the ribbon from slipping out of the hardware.

what you need

Sewing Kit (page 21)

2 white or light-colored slips

Commercial fabric dye and dyeing supplies (page 15)

2 yards (1.8 m) of lace, 2½ inches (6.4 cm) wide

1 yard (0.9 m) of decorative ribbon per slip, the same width as the slip straps

Basic screen-printing kit (optional)

•

Sizes vary

Seam allowance ¼ inch (6 mm)

5

Add any designs you like with a screen-printing kit, available at most arts and crafts stores or online. First prepare your slip by pulling it over a piece of cardboard to make it flat, then follow the manufacturer's instructions to screen-print.

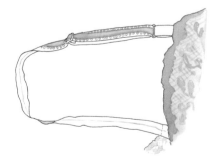

figure 1

They always said you'd break hearts. You fall in love easily and wear your heart on your sleeve, but this time—with a killer tank and boxer set—it's for keeps.

heartbreaker

What You Do

1

Enlarge the templates on pages 124-125. On folded fabric, cut out the pieces. For the drawstring, cut a strip of fabric 1½ x 60 inches (3.8 cm x 1.5 m).

TANK TOP

1

Trace the small heart template onto the fusible web. Cut it out, leaving a border of approximately ½ inch (1.3 cm) around the shape.

2

Press the heart shape onto the back of a small piece of the cotton fabric, following the manufacturer's instructions. Cut it out on the line you traced.

3

Press the heart onto the middle front of the tank top, about 2 inches (5.1 cm) from the top edge.

4

Pin a piece of tear-away stabilizer behind the heart on the underside of the fabric. Stitch around the heart using a machine buttonhole stitch and a machine needle for stretch knits. Remove the stabilizer.

SHORTS

1

With right sides facing, stitch the fronts together at the center front seam. Do the same with the backs. Overlock/serge the edges and press.

(continued on next page)

what you need

Sewing Kit (page 21)

Serger

Cotton fabric for shorts and heart sachet, 45 inches (1.1 m) wide
XS, S: 1¼ yards (1.1 m)
M, L, XL: 1⅜ yards (1.3 m)

2 yards (1.8 m) of ribbon or cord for the drawstring (optional)

7 x 9-inch (17.8 x 22.9 cm) piece of paper-backed fusible web

Purchased tank top

5 x 6-inch (12.7 x 15.2 cm) piece of tear-away fabric stabilizer

5 x 6-inch (12.7 x 15.2 cm) scrap of red fabric for the heart sachet

3 x 4-inch (7.6 x 10.2 cm) scrap of muslin

1 tablespoon (14.3 g) of dried lavender or other scented herb

10 inches (25.4 cm) of cord, ⅛ inch (3 mm) wide

Small quantity of fiberfill or other stuffing material

2 x 4-inch (5.1 x 10.2 cm) piece of fusible interfacing

1½ yards (1.4 m) of elastic, ½ inch (1.3 cm) wide, or length to fit your waist measurement

Sized for XS, S, M, L, XL

Seam allowance ¼ inch (6 mm)

With right sides facing, pin the front to the back, matching the outside seams. Stitch both side seams and overlock the edges. Matching the center front seam to the center back seam, stitch the inside leg. Overlock the edges and press.

Turn the shorts right side out. Using a ruler and dressmaker's chalk, make a mark ¼ inch (6 mm) from the top edge, then measure down 1⅜ inches (3.5 cm) and make another mark. These will be the fold lines for the casing. Mark the buttonholes ½ inch (1.3 cm) from the center seam on both sides, 2¼ inches (5.7 cm) from the top, and another ½ inch (1.3 cm) to the bottom of the buttonhole (see figure 2, page 83).

Cut two 2 x 2-inch (5.1 x 5.1 cm) pieces of fusible interfacing and iron them to the wrong side of the fabric, centered behind the buttonhole marks, following the manufacturer's instructions. Make two ½-inch (1.3 cm) buttonholes as marked and carefully cut them open.

To complete the casing, turn the shorts wrong side out. Press under the top edge ¼ inch (6 mm), and press under another 1⅜ inches (3.5 cm). Edgestitch the casing in place. For the ruffled effect at the top of the casing, stitch ¼ inch (6 mm) from the top edge, all the way around.

To make the drawstring, with wrong sides facing, fold the 60-inch (1.5) strip in half lengthwise and press. Open up the strip and press both sides into the center. Refold along the center and press again to make a strip that is about ⅜ inch (1 cm) wide. Stitch the long folded edge, tucking in the ends and stitching around the corners.

Measure your waist and cut a piece of elastic to fit, making it ¾ inch (1.9 cm) longer than your comfortable waist measurement. With a safety pin attached to one end of the elastic, thread it into the casing through one buttonhole and out the other. Overlap the ends of the elastic about ¾ inch (1.9 cm) and stitch them securely together. Adjust the elastic so it is entirely within the waist casing. Thread one end of the drawstring through the casing in the same way. Even the gathers around the waist and make sure the drawstring is even on both sides. Anchor the drawstring and elastic in place by sewing through all layers on the waist casing at the back center seam.

Turn the shorts wrong side out. Press under ¼ inch (6 mm) on both leg hems, and press under another 1 inch (2.5 cm). Edgestitch the hems in place.

HEART SACHET

Trace the small heart template onto the fusible web. Cut it out, leaving a border of approximately ½ inch (1.3 cm) around the shape.

figure 1

2

Press the heart shape onto the back of the red scrap fabric. Cut it out on the line you traced.

3

Press the small heart to the middle of a large heart. Stitch around the inner heart using a machine buttonhole stitch.

4

Fold the muslin in half and stitch two sides to form a little pocket. Fill with lavender and stitch the open side closed.

5

Fold the piece of cord in half and position it on the front of the appliquéd heart (figure 1). Baste in place.

6

With right rides facing, stitch the two large heart shapes together, leaving a 2-inch (5.1 cm) gap on one side for turning. Clip the curves and turn right side out. Press lightly. Stuff with fiberfill and insert the lavender bag in the middle of the stuffing. Hand-sew the opening closed.

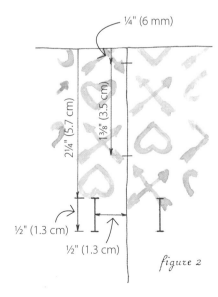

¼" (6 mm)

2¼" (5.7 cm)

1⅜" (3.5 cm)

½" (1.3 cm)

½" (1.3 cm)

figure 2

cupcake cami

Comfy, cute, and cool—
that's what this cami is all
about. Whip one up and
you'll be ready to settle down for
the afternoon with a romantic movie
and your favorite sweet thing.

What You Do

Cut out the pattern pieces and cut out the front and back from the rib knit.

2
Cut a piece of fold-over elastic to fit the top edge of the cami back. Cut a strip of fusible web tape to the same length. Lay the unfolded elastic flat, wrong side up, and fuse the tape along one long edge of the elastic, following the manufacturer's instructions. Remove the paper backing. Align the top of the cami back, wrong side down, on the fusible tape. Fuse in place. With the fabric right side up, fold the elastic over the top edge of the fabric as you stitch it in place. Use a small zigzag stitch with one side of the stitch falling just off the edge of the elastic.

3
Cut a piece of stretch lace to fit the top edge of the cami front. Cut a strip of fusible web tape to the same length. Lay the front of the cami right side up on the ironing board and fuse the tape to the top edge. Remove the paper backing. Align the stretch lace, right side up, with the tape (see figure 1 on page 86). Fuse the lace in place. With the fabric right side up, stitch the stretch lace to the fabric, using a wide zigzag stitch.

4
With right sides together, match up the sides of the cami and stitch, using a very narrow zigzag stitch (or serger). Press the seams open.

(continued on next page)

what you need

Sewing Kit (page 21)

⅔ yard (61 cm) of tubular rib knit

1⅔ yards (1.5 m) of fold-over elastic, ⅝ inch (1.6 cm) wide

1 package of paper-backed fusible web tape, ¼ inch (6 mm) wide

1¼ yards (1.1 m) of stretch lace, 1¼ inches (3.2 cm) wide

Tissue paper (optional)

Sized for XS, S, and M

Seam allowance ¼ inch (6 mm)

designer • **LORETTA GJELTEMA**

Color Choice

You'll find that fold-over elastic comes in an attractive range of colors. But if you're not finding just the right shade, you can buy white lace and elastic, and dye them to match (page 15).

For the armholes and straps, cut two strips of fold-over elastic to your size:

> XS: 24½ inches (62.2 cm)
> S: 24¾ inches (62.9 cm)
> M: 25¼ inches (64.1 cm)

With the unfolded elastic right sides together, stitch the ends of each strap piece together to form two circular strips. You may find it helpful to place a piece of tissue paper under the elastic as you sew (then tear it away and discard). Press the seam allowances open.

6

Pin the front and back pattern pieces to the surface of the ironing board (or another padded surface) with side seams overlapping. With right sides facing, fold the cami and center the side seam over the pattern, pinning it in place. This keeps the cami from stretching as you then apply fusible strips along the armhole edge (figure 2).

Turn the pattern pieces over and pin them down again. Pin the other side of the folded cami to the pattern, and apply fusible strips as in step 6. Unpin the cami and set the pattern aside.

8

Using the elastic strips you made in step 5, place one strip flat, wrong side up, on the ironing board. Remove the paper backing from the tape on one armhole. Aligning the seams of the elastic and the cami, place the cami right side up over the elastic. Match the edge of the cami to the fold line of the elastic (figure 3). Press to fuse, being careful not to stretch the cami or the elastic. With the fabric right side up, fold the elastic over the top edge of the fabric as you stitch it in place, using a small zigzag stitch. As you reach the strap area, continue stitching the sides of the elastic around the circle. Repeat for the other side of the cami.

9

Measure the entire bottom edge of the cami (both sides). Subtract 2 inches (5.1 cm) from the measurement and cut a strip of stretch lace to that length. With right sides together, stitch the ends of the lace to form a circle. Press the seam allowance open. (Once again, tissue paper may be helpful.)

10

Mark one edge of the stretch lace in quarters (with one mark at the side seam), then mark the lower edge of the cami in quarters (with one mark at each side seam). With both the cami and the lace right side up, pin the lace to the cami at the quarter marks, aligning side seams. Stretching the lace as you go (to match the length of the cami), stitch the lace to the cami, using either a three-step or a standard zigzag stitch. The cami will gather slightly at the lower edge.

figure 1

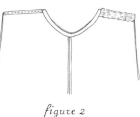

figure 2

figure 3

ou know how to win a pillow fight without messing up your hair, and this silk romper was designed with you in mind. It's playful and kittenish, but sophisticated too, with a sexy halter that shows off your back.

trixie

what you need

Sewing Kit (page 21)

1 yard (0.9 m) of muslin

Washable marker or dressmaker's pencil

Dressmaker's curve

1½ yards (1.4 m) of silk A for the romper

½ yard (45.7 cm) of silk B
for the contrasting bands and tie

3 yards (2.7 m) of ribbon, ½ inch (1.3 cm) wide

1 yard (0.9 m) of elastic, 1 inch (2.5 cm) wide

•

Adjustable size

Seam allowance ⅝ inch (1.6 cm)

What You Do

1

Take your own measurements to make this garment.

For the bodice:

- Measure from armpit to armpit across the bust line and add 4 inches (10.2 cm) plus 1¼ inches (3.2 cm) for two seam allowances (one on either side).
- Measure from the breastbone to the waist and add 4 inches (10.2 cm) plus 1¼ inches (3.2 cm) for two seam allowances.
- Cut a piece to these measurements from silk A. With chalk or tape, mark which side is the top.

For the shorts:

- While seated, measure your crotch depth from waist to chair along the side of your body and add 5 inches (12.7 cm) plus 1¼ inches (3.2 cm) for two seam allowances.
- Measure around the widest part of your hips and add 8 inches. Divide by 2, and add 1¼ inches (3.2 cm) for two seam allowances.
- Use these measurements to make both the front and the back of the shorts (see box on page 91).

From silk B, cut four pieces, as listed below. Depending on the width of your fabric and the size of your garment, you may need to cut some or all of them as two pieces and stitch them together. If so, remember to add the additional ⅝-inch (1.6 cm) seam allowances you'll need to make a continuous band or tie. Stitch as needed and press the seams open.

- Cut two leg bands that are 2½ inches (6.4 cm) x the finished width of your shorts, plus 1¼ inches (3.2 cm) for two seam allowances.
- Cut a waistband that is 2½ inches (6.4 cm) x the finished width of the top of the shorts, plus 1¼ inches (3.2 cm) for two seam allowances.
- Cut a tie that is 6 x 60 inches (15.2 cm x 1.5 m).

Make a narrow hem at each side of the bodice by pressing under ¼ inch (6 mm), then pressing under another ¼ inch (6 mm). Stitch in place. Make the casing at the top by pressing under ¼ inch (6 mm) and then another 2 inches (5.1 cm). Edgestitch the casing in place.

With right sides facing, stitch the front of the shorts together at the center seam. Do the same for the back. (Because the pieces are the same, it doesn't matter which you choose for the front and back.) Clip the curves and press the seams open. With right sides facing, stitch the front and back together at the crotch seam. Stitch the side seams as well, leaving the top ⅝ inch (1.6 cm) of the seam open. Make a narrow hem along the top edge of the back of the shorts, from side seam to side seam, by pressing under ¼ inch (6 mm) twice. Stitch a narrow hem at the bottom edge of the shorts legs.

Trixie's Choice

Since this isn't a fitted garment, you can adjust the amount of gathering in the legs as well as at the neckline, making the romper as roomy as you like. Also, if you'd like a little more coverage, you can experiment with extending the bodice out a bit toward the back of the waist rather than placing it flush with the side seams of the shorts.

5

Press under each long edge of the leg bands ¼ inch (6 mm), and then press under the ends ⅝ inch (1.6 cm). Pin each band to the right side of a pant leg, 2 inches (5.1 cm) above the hem. Position the pressed edges to meet at the side seam of the pants; you'll leave both ends open to form a casing for the ribbon. Stitch the bands in place along the long edges.

6

Fold the bottom of the bodice and mark where the center is located. Make a row of gathering stitches along this edge. With right sides facing, pin the bodice to the front of the pants, matching the center of the bodice to the center front seam, and placing the hemmed edges at the side seams. Gather to fit. Stitch in place and press the seam allowance toward the pants.

7

Stitch the ends of the waistband together to make a continuous loop, and press the seams open. Press under each long edge ¼ inch (6 mm), and pin it to the waist along the seamline of the front and the pressed edge of the back. Edgestitch each long edge, leaving an opening to insert the elastic.

8

With right sides facing, fold the tie in half lengthwise and stitch, leaving one end open. Turn right side out through the open end and turn under the raw edges. Press the tie and slipstitch the opening.

9

Cut two pieces of ribbon that are each the circumference of your upper leg plus about 20 inches (50.8 cm). Thread each through the leg bands, gather as desired, and tie.

10

Cut the elastic to the desired length and thread through the waistband. Overlap the elastic ends and stitch together securely. Stitch the opening in the waistband closed.

Making the Shorts Pattern

- Draw a rectangle on muslin to the size of your measurements, as described in step 1.
- Add the curve of the crotch by first marking 5 ⅝ inches (14.3 cm) from the bottom, along one long edge of the rectangle.
- Mark 4 inches (10.2 cm) to the right from this point, and make a gentle arc from the waist to this spot, using the dressmaker's curve.
- Extend the rectangle as shown (figure 1).
- Fold silk A and cut two pieces from the muslin pattern. Flip the pattern over, place it back on the fabric, and cut two more pieces.

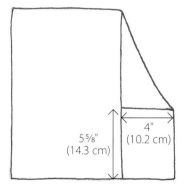

5 ⅝" (14.3 cm)   4" (10.2 cm)

figure 1

11

Thread the tie through the bodice casing and tie as desired.

G o ahead, admire away! Stretch fabric flatters any figure, and the flirty cut of these pant- ies will make you want to shake your booty.

narcissus

What You Do

1

Enlarge the templates on page 120 and cut the pieces from the four-way stretch fabric. Cut a second crotch piece from the cotton jersey.

2

With wrong sides facing, pin the two crotch pieces together. With right sides of the stretch fabric facing, line up the narrow end with the front piece. Pin, then serge the seam.

3

With right sides of the stretch fabric facing, pin the wider end of the crotch to the back. Pin, then serge the seam.

4

Serge the lace onto the two top edges and leg holes of the panties (figure 1).

5

With right sides facing, line up the side seams and serge both sides of the panties together. Turn the panties right side out and secure the thread ends.

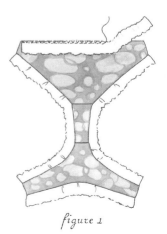

figure 1

what you need

Sewing Kit (page 21)

Serger

⅜ yard (34.3 cm) of four-way stretch fabric

⅛ yard (11.4 cm) of
four-way stretch cotton jersey

Stretch lace trim, 1½ inches (3.8 cm) wide:
S: 2 yards (1.8 m)
M: 2¼ yards (2.1 m)
L: 2½ yards (2.3 m)

Sized for XS, S, M

Seam allowance ⅛ inch (3 mm)

designer • ELISE OLSON

evening delicacies

savor the
evening in
something
unforgettable

*M*ake some sparks with this cami
and the evening is sure to heat up.

What You Do

1

Cut out the pattern pieces and set them aside. For the body of the camisole, cut a piece of lace fabric to one of the following lengths:

> S: 26 inches (66 cm)
> M: 28 inches (71.1 cm)
> L: 30 inches (76.2 cm)

2

Fold this piece of fabric in half and mark the center edge (on the fold) with a pin. On each side of the pin, ½ inch (1.3 cm) away, use the cup cutout template to trace two semicircle shapes (see figure 1 on page 98). Cut them out.

3

Line up the straight edge of the cup pattern with the straight edge of the remaining lace. Before you cut, make sure you've allowed room to cut out four pieces. Cut one, then flip the pattern over, move it to the other side of the lace, and cut out an opposite cup piece (see figure 2 on page 98). Cut two more in the same way.

4

With right sides facing, pair up two opposing cup pieces and serge together. Repeat with the other pair.

5

Check the body for fit by placing the cup cutouts under your bra and wrapping the cami snuggly around your torso. Trim to fit, if necessary; keep the back seam centered by trimming the same amount off of each end. With right sides facing, serge the back seam. Turn right side out.

what you need

Sewing Kit (page 21)

Serger

Stretch lace, 6 inches (15.2 cm) wide:
S: 1¼ yards (1.1 m)
M: 1½ yards (1.4 m)
L: 1¾ yards (1.6 m)

1¼ yards (1.1 m) of plush
elastic strapping, ⅜ inch (1 cm) wide

2 pairs of bra adjusters
(rings and slides), ⅜ inch (1 cm) wide

Sized for XS, S, M

Seam allowance ⅛ inch (3 mm)

figure 1

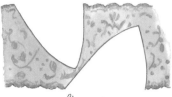

figure 2

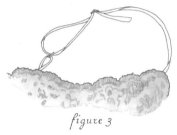

figure 3

6

One at a time, with the cami wrong side out and with right sides facing, position a sewn cup into a cup cutout, making sure that both ends of the cup align with the cutout. Serge each cup in place. Turn the cami right side out and secure the thread ends.

7

Cut the elastic strapping into two 18-inch (45.7 cm) pieces and two 4-inch (10.2 cm) pieces. Fold under one end of a long piece slightly to make it neat, and center it on the top point of one of the cups. With a sewing machine, stitch over the strap a couple of times to secure it. Repeat with the other long strap and cup.

8

To find where the back strap will be attached, lay the cami flat with the cups facing down and the back seam centered and facing up. Place two pins on the top edge of the back where it intersects each cup's center seam. Slide one of the rings over a 4-inch (10.2 cm) piece of strapping and fold the strap in half at the ring. Fold under both ends of the strap slightly, and stitch them to one of the pinned locations on the wrong side. Attach the other short strap in the same way.

9

Fit a slide onto one of the long straps and slip it along the strap a bit. Thread the strapping through the corresponding ring and then back under and through the slide (figure 3). Pull this end through the slide about 1½ inches (3.8 cm) and then fold it under slightly and stitch it to itself in a square shape, going over it a couple of times to reinforce. Repeat with the other strap.

sassafras

his 1940s-inspired garter belt fuses all things girly and burlesque in one little laced-up number. Cream cotton lace and satin ribbon ties will tease out your fantasy and tickle your fancy.

what you need

Sewing Kit (page 21)

½ yard (45.7 cm) of silk dupioni, cotton, or fabric of choice

20 inches (50.8 cm) of matching or contrasting fabric to make bias binding or 1 yard (0.9 m) of 1-inch (2.5 cm) single-fold or ½-inch (1.3 cm) double-fold bias tape

10 inches (25.4 cm) of fusible interfacing

39½ inches (1 m) of narrow elastic

78¾ inches (2 m) of plastic boning

78¾ inches (2 m) of fine cream cotton lace, about 2 to 2¾ inches (5.1 to 7 cm) wide

24 grommets, size 00, or two-part eyelets, ³⁄₁₆ inch (5 mm) wide

Grommet-setting tools (either hammer set or setting pliers)

157½ inches (4 m) of narrow double-faced satin ribbon

4 suspenders/garters or elastic and suspender components

Adjustable size

Seam allowance ½ inch (1.3 cm) unless otherwise noted

What You Do

Enlarge the templates on pages 126-127. Before cutting any fabric, make necessary adjustments to the template for size (see Custom Sizing box on page 101). Cut out the pieces as indicated on the templates. If making your own bias binding (page 32), cut strips 2 inches (5.1 cm) wide and stitch them together to make 1 yard (0.9 m) of binding. Use a bias tape maker or press by hand to make the amount of tape needed.

Fuse the interfacing to the wrong side of each facing and reinforcement piece.

Press under ½ inch (1.3 cm) on each long side of the reinforcement triangles (not the top or bottom edges). Pin the reinforcements in place, lining up the bottom shapes, and topstitch onto the main pieces.

Press under the longest side of each facing piece ½ inch (1.3 cm) and stitch to form a narrow hem. With right sides together, pin the opposite edge of each facing to the sides of the front and back. Stitch and press the seams.

Form boning channels by stitching a line approximately ½ inch (1.3 cm) inside each side of the triangles, or just wide enough to accommodate your boning. Do the same ½ inch (1.3 cm) from each side seam (see figure 2 on page 101).

Press under a ½-inch (1.3 cm) hem along the top edge of both front and back pieces. At one side of a top edge, pin the narrow elastic over the raw edge. Stretch the elastic a bit as you attach it with a zigzag stitch (see figure 3 on page 102).

Cut the boning to the appropriate length for all your boning channels, leaving a space of about ¼ inch (6 mm) at the bottom of each channel (figure 2). Insert the boning and trim any sharp edges (page 19).

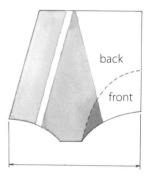

figure 1

Hip measurement, divided by 4, and minus 1 inch (2.5 cm)

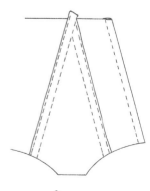

figure 2

Custom Sizing

The template is sized to fit 40-inch (101.6 cm) hips. Applied to the template: 40 inches (101.6 cm) is divided by 4 (representing four pieces for front and back), minus 1 inch (2.5 cm), to allow for the lacings. The result is 9 inches (22.9 cm) from the furthest point on the left to the center fold on the right (figure 1).

Measure around your hips, about 7 inches (17.8 cm) below your waist. Use this measurement to adapt the template, dividing by 4 and subtracting 1 inch (2.5 cm). Add or subtract from the sides and center of both the front and the back templates, as needed. To make a longer or shorter garment body, add or subtract from the top edge. You may want to cut the body shape out of scrap fabric first to check that the proportions are correct for your size. Remember to allow for a gap at each hip to show off the lacing.

Stitch the bias binding to the bottom edge of both front and back. Hand-sew the cotton lace to the wrong side, along the stitched edge of the bias tape. Gather by making little folds every ½ inch (1.3 cm) or so as you stitch.

Set grommets (page 20) down all four outside edges, 6 per side and evenly spaced, inside the boning.

Cut the narrow ribbon into two strips of equal length. With a front and back edge side by side, starting at the bottom, thread narrow ribbon up to the top and down again in a criss-cross manner. Tie a bow at the bottom. Lace both sides, then check for fit. Make adjustments as needed. Leave the ribbon ends long to allow for loosening the sides when removing the garment. **Note:** Single-sided ribbon will fray, so be sure to use double-sided ribbon as specified.

The ruffled suspenders are optional, because you could use purchased ones as they are. For that extra touch of vintage elegance, however, do the following (figure 4):

- Cut strips of your chosen fabric 1½ times the length of the suspender elastic and about 2½ times the width.
- Fold each strip in half lengthwise, right sides together, and stitch the raw edges together.
- Turn each strip right side out and press with the seam centered down one side.
- Edgestitch down both folded edges, being sure to leave enough room to thread the elastic through.
- Carefully dismantle one purchased suspender at a time, because it's easy to forget how to put them back together.
- Insert each elastic suspender strap, pulling the elastic as you go to ruffle the fabric. Stitch both ends to secure the fabric.
- Reassemble the suspenders and then stitch them in position at the base of the reinforced areas of the suspender belt.

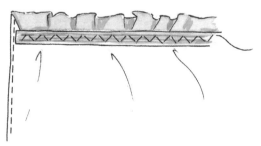

figure 3

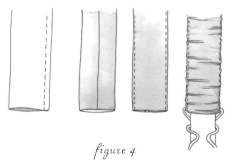

figure 4

Slip into soft organic cotton and laze the day away. This chemise is as comfy as your favorite Tee, but about ten times cuter.

Serena

Sewing Knit Fabrics

For best results when sewing knit fabrics, try some of these strategies:

- Shorten the length of your straight stitch to 10 stitches per inch (2.5 cm).
- Change the machine needle to a ball-point or stretch needle.
- Use ballpoint or silk straight pins.

What You Do

1

Cut out the pattern pieces. (The pattern is a S/M. To increase the size, add width at the side seams.) To prevent mistakes, make paper templates for each separate piece (four in the front, four in the back) before cutting your fabric (see figure 1 on page 106). Label each piece clearly, so none gets accidentally flipped over or confused with similar pieces.

For the shoulder ties, make a 1½ x 18-inch (3.8 x 45.7 cm) pattern and cut four ties. From the interfacing, cut one front and one back.

2

To attach the interfacing, aligning the edges, pin the front interfacing to the wrong side of the upper front fabric piece. Baste the armhole and side seams, just shy of the ½-inch (1.3 cm) seam allowance. Trim the seam allowance of the interfacing only, close to the basting stitches. Repeat for the back interfacing and upper back fabric piece.

3

To stitch the side seams, start with the upper front and upper back pieces. With right sides facing and edges aligned, pin and stitch together the side seams. Finish the seam allowances. Repeat for the middle front/back and lower front/back.

what you need

Sewing Kit (page 21)

Ballpoint sewing machine needle size 70/10 or 75/11

Large sheets or rolls of paper

2¼ yards (2.1 m) of organic cotton single knit, 44 to 60 inches (1.1 to 1.5 m) wide

½ yard (45.7 cm) of lightweight woven or nonwoven interfacing

Sized for S/M

Seam allowance ½ inch (1.3 cm) unless otherwise noted

4

To hem the edges, working with each section individually (upper, middle, and lower), turn under and pin ½ inch (1.3 cm) to the wrong side of the fabric at the hemline. Stretch and stitch a lettuce edge along the hem of each section (see box on page 107).

5

To make the shoulder ties, fold one strip in half lengthwise and pin. Starting at the folded edge, stitch along one short end and then down the length of the tie, aligning the folded edge with the edge of your presser foot (figure 2). This will cre-

ate a narrow ¼-inch (6 mm) tube. Finish the seam allowance with a triple zigzag and trim. With the help of a tube turner (page 23), turn the tie right side out. The narrow seam allowance will fill the void inside the tube. Repeat for all the ties.

6

To assemble the chemise, with right sides of both fabrics facing out, pin the upper front and back to the middle front and back. Pin along the neckline and armhole edges, and pin the cutends of the ties to the shoulder edges (figure 3). To prevent the tie ends from catching in seams where they shouldn't, coil them neatly and safety pin the coils to the body of the nightie out of the way of the seams. Machine-baste both layers and the ends of the ties, stitching just shy of ½ inch (1.3 cm). Do not clean-finish or trim the seam allowance.

7

For the last layer, with right sides facing, pin the lower front/ back to the assembled upper and middle pieces. Stitch the neckline and armhole edges, catching the ties at the shoulder edges. Keep a ½-inch (1.3 cm) seam allowance throughout, except for stitching ¼ inch (6 mm) through the tie ends (figure 4). Finish the seam allowances and turn the nightie right side out. Understitch through both middle and lower sections, close to the seamline along the lower curves of the armholes.

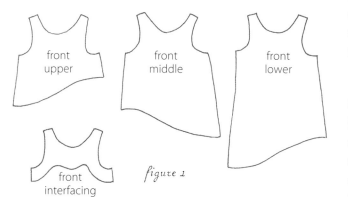

front upper

front middle

front lower

front interfacing

figure 1

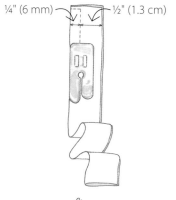

¼" (6 mm)   ½" (1.3 cm)

figure 2

figure 3

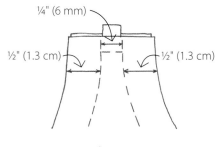

¼" (6 mm)

½" (1.3 cm)   ½" (1.3 cm)

figure 4

gardenia

Finishing the Seams

Clean-finish the seam allowance through both layers of fabric with a three-step zigzag stitch close to the seam. To prevent tunneling, avoid a one-step zigzag. Trim the seam allowance close to the seam finish and press the seam to one side.

Stitching a Lettuce-Edged Hem

To achieve the distinctive ruffled edge featured in this project, practice the following on scrap pieces of the organic cotton knit before stitching your nightie:

- Set the machine to a regular one-step zigzag (not a triple zigzag). Use a medium or wide stitch width, and a short or medium stitch length.
- Position the folded edge of the fabric under the presser foot.
- With one hand behind the presser foot and the other hand in front, stretch the folded edge of the fabric as you stitch along the fold, allowing the right-hand swing of the zigzag to fall off the folded edge. The stitches will distort the fabric, causing it to ripple and curve.
- When finished stitching, carefully trim the loose seam allowance, stretching the fabric again as you trim.

This little silk bustier can't be stopped, although you may end up stopping traffic. All you have to do is dare to bare—and channel your inner siren.

What You Do

1

Cut out the pattern pieces and cut out the fabric pieces. Keep track of the pieces by labeling each one in the seam allowance (see the mirror image box on page 40). Mark hemlines and dots.

2

To make the tie:

- With right sides facing, pin the wide end of an A piece to the wide end of B piece, and stitch (see figure 1 on page 110). Repeat with the remaining A and B pieces, to make four joined sections.
- With right sides facing, stitch two joined sections together, starting at the dot on B and stopping at the dot on A. Turn right side out and press. Repeat with the other two joined sections.

3

To make the front of the bustier, below the ties:

- Make a narrow hem at the top of C, as marked on the template. Set aside.
- With right sides facing, stitch the bottom of a right-hand D to the top of a right-hand E. Press the seam toward D. Repeat with the left-hand D and E. (The remaining D pieces will be used later as facing.)
- With right sides facing, stitch the right-hand D/E piece to the right side of C. Press the seams toward the sides. Stitch the left-hand D/E piece to the other side of C and press (see figure 2 on page 110).

what you need

Sewing Kit (page 21)

Zipper foot

1⅜ yards (1.3 m) of dupioni silk

1½ yards (1.4 m) of covered boning, ½ inch (1.3 cm) wide

10-inch (25.4 cm) separating zipper

1 hook and eye

Sized for XS, S, M, L

Seam allowance ⅝ inch (1.6 cm) unless otherwise noted

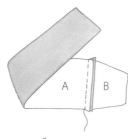

figure 1

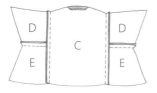

figure 2

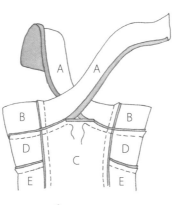

figure 3

To attach the tie to the front, with right sides facing and the long end in the center, pin the unstitched lower edge of one tie to the left or right top of the front, matching side seams. Pin the other tie to the opposite side. Stitch both in place and press the seams toward the tie (figure 3). Leave the opening as is for now.

To make the back:

- With right sides facing, stitch the bottom of a right-hand F to the top of a right-hand G. Press the seam toward F. Repeat with a left-hand F and G. Put the remaining F pieces aside to use later for facing.
- With right sides facing, stitch the bottom of a right-hand H to the top of a right-hand I. Press the seam toward H. Repeat with a left-hand H and I. Put the remaining H pieces aside.
- With right sides facing, stitch the correct H/I piece to the correct F/G piece, checking the templates for guidance. Press the seams toward H/I (figure 4).

To attach the front and back, with right sides facing, pin the front of the bustier to the back pieces at the side seams. Stitch both sides. Try the bustier on for size, and adjust the seams as needed. Hem the bottom by pressing under ¼ inch (6 mm), and then another 1¼ inches (3.2 cm), adjusting for fullness as needed. Stitch the hem and press.

cosmo bustier

To make the facings:

- On both remaining D pieces, press under the "stitch to C" side ⅝ inch (1.6 cm).
- Lift the unstitched edges of the tie, and with right sides facing, stitch each D facing piece to a B facing piece. Press the seams toward B.
- Stitch each F facing to the correct H facing. Press the seams open.
- Stitch the H side of each facing to the B and D facing (figure 5).

To add the boning:

- Measure the length of the facing's side seam and of the facing's back seam. Add 1 inch (2.5 cm) to each measurement. Cut two pieces of covered boning for each length.
- Slide back the casing on the ends of all cut pieces and trim back ⅝ inch (1.6 cm), rounding the edges.
- Matching the casings with boning to the correct seams, center each casing over each seam and pin. Baste across the upper and lower edges of the casing, and stitch close to the long edges.
- Pin the facing in place at the top edge, aligning seams, and stitch (figure 6). Understitch the facing to the seam allowance as far as you can.

To add the zipper:

- Turn the facing to the inside. Press under the lower edge of the facing ⅝ inch (1.6 cm).
- Lift the facings out of the way, and with right sides together, baste the center back seams. Press the seam open.
- On the wrong side, center the closed zipper facedown over the basted seam, with the zipper stop positioned about ¾ inch (1.9 cm) below the top seam. Baste through the zipper tape on both sides of the zipper.
- On the outside, stitch along the basting through all thicknesses, using a zipper foot. Remove the basting.
- Replace the back lining and turn under the side raw edge to clear the zipper teeth. Hand-sew in place.

To finish, hand-sew the rest of the lining in place. Hand-sew a hook and eye above the zipper. Tie the ends of the bodice in a bow.

- On the outside, stitch along the basting through all thicknesses, using a zipper foot. Remove the basting.
- Replace the back lining and turn under the side raw edge to clear the zipper teeth. Hand-sew in place.

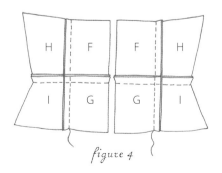

figure 4

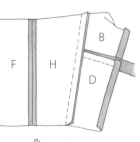

figure 5

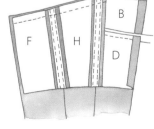

figure 6

Bridesmaid or belle of the ball? In this garter, you decide. Shiny silk and embroidered satin ribbon will give you a leg up on the competition. What's your secret?

What You Do

1

Measure around your thigh, above the knee where you plan to wear the garter. You want the garter to fit snugly, but not too tightly. Add about 1 inch (2.5 cm), and cut the elastic.

2

Cut a strip of silk 3¼ inches (8.3 cm) wide and twice the length of the elastic.

3

With right sides together, stitch the fabric down one long side. It should be just wide enough to encase the elastic. Turn right side out and press with the seam in the center of one side of the strip. Hand-sew the lace along the seamline so it hangs down below the garter (figure 1).

4

Thread the elastic through the silk casing. Secure each end with several passes of machine stitching, and even out the gathers. Overlap the ends by about 1 inch (2.5 cm) and stitch the ends together, keeping the lace ends tidy.

5

To make the bow, enlarge the template on page 121 and cut a rectangle of silk. Trace the design onto your silk and embroider it. For the stems, use stem stitch; use straight stitch and satin stitch to embroider the leaves; do the petals in chain stitch; and make dainty little French knots for the flower centers (see page 33). Fold the piece to form the loops of the bow. There's no need to finish the edges, because they will be hidden.

6

Cut the satin ribbon to make a folded loop slightly wider than the embroidered loop. Place it behind the embroidered piece and stitch the two together in the center.

what you need

Sewing Kit (page 21)

½ yard (45.7 cm) of soft elastic,
1¼ inches (3.2 cm) wide

½ yard (45.7 cm) of silk dupioni

1 yard (0.9 m) of fine cream cotton
lace, 2½ to 3 inches (6.4 to 7.6 cm) wide

Embroidery floss in two coordinating colors

½ yard (45.7 cm) of double-faced
satin ribbon, 1⅜ inches (3.5 cm) wide

Size is adjustable

Seam allowance ¼ inch (6 mm)

7

To make the "knot" of the bow, cut a strip of ribbon 2½ to 3 inches (6.4 to 7.6 cm) long. Cut a 1¾-inch-wide (4.4 cm) strip of silk the same length. Press under the sides of the silk by about ¼ inch (6 mm) to make the strip just under 1¼ inches (3.2 cm) wide. Place the ribbon behind the silk, with the edges showing on either side. Wrap both around the center of the main bow. Stitch to hold together. Hand-sew the bow to the garter, using small stitches under the bow.

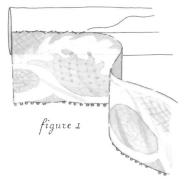

figure 1

strawberry

You take your coffee black, but with plenty of sugar, and these are the hipsters for you. Stretch lace hugs every curve, and a sexy little ribbon ties in the back.

what you need

Sewing Kit (page 21)

Serger

Stretch lace, 4 inches (10.2 cm) wide:
S: 1⅛ yards (1 m)
M, L: 1¼ yards (1.1 m)

⅛ yard (11.4 cm) of stretch cotton jersey

Satin ribbon, ¼ inch (6 mm) wide:
S: 42 inches (1.1 m)
M: 46 inches (1.2 m)
L: 50 inches (1.3 m)

Anti-fraying glue

Sized for XS, S, M

Seam allowance ⅛ inch (3 mm)

What You Do

1

Enlarge the templates on page 122. Cut out the pieces from the stretch lace and cut a second crotch piece from the cotton jersey. Cut the satin ribbon in half and apply anti-fraying glue to all four ends.

2

With right sides facing, serge both crotch pieces together along the sides. Turn right side out.

3

With right sides facing, serge the two body pieces together at the ends. Turn the body right side out with the seams in the center. Lay the piece flat so that it resembles a V. (Since the front and back of the panties are the same, it doesn't matter which side faces up.)

4

With right sides facing, center the crotch along the seam, with one end at the point of the V. The point will stick out a little beyond the crotch (figure 1). Serge the seam. Attach the other side of the crotch in the same way.

5

Fold under one end of a ribbon slightly to make it neat, and pin it about 1 inch (2.5 cm) from the side of the panties in the back. Position the ribbon more or less horizontally, with the loose end facing the center of the back. Using a sewing machine, stitch the end in place. Attach the other ribbon to the opposite side of the back, in the same way. Turn the panties right side out and secure the thread ends.

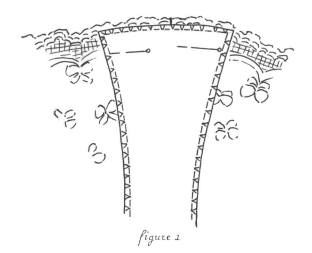

figure 1

117

Y ou can wish on
the heavens,
but in metallic
satin spandex, *you'll* be the
brightest star. Choose your
own special graphic image
for an extra dose of divine.

What You Do

1

Enlarge the templates on page 128 and cut out the pattern pieces. Lay them on the fabric with the stretch running from left to right. Trace and cut out.

PANTIES

1

With right sides together and using a flatlock stitch, merge the side seams of the panties. Stretch the seam apart so it lays flat.

2

Using an overlock stitch, trim all edges of the panties. Cast off at the seams. Finish the panties by knotting off the wooly nylon ends and trimming them short.

CAMI

1

With right sides together, and using a two-thread converter and a flatlock stitch, merge the back seam of the cami. Stretch the seam apart so it lays flat.

2

Using an overlock stitch, trim all edges of the cami. Cast off at the seams and at the base of the armholes. Finish the bra by knotting off the wooly nylon ends and trimming them short.

3

Cut out two patch images. On a piece of large scrap paper, spray the back side of the patches with the machine embroidery spray. Position each patch wherever you like on the cami and panties, and press to stick it on. With a sewing machine, stitch around the patches using a small zigzag stitch. It helps to stop the needle in the down position to pivot the seams.

what you need

Sewing Kit (page 21)

Serger with flatlock capabilities and a two-thread converter

Two-way satin spandex stretch fabric, 60 inches (1.5 m) wide:
XS/S: 1 yard (0.9 m)
S/M, M/L: 1½ yards (1.4 m)

Basic screen-printing kit (optional)

Two graphic images screen-printed onto stretch fabric (may be cut from a jersey T-shirt)

Disappearing spray fabric adhesive for machine embroidery

Sized for XS/S, S/M, M/L

Seam allowance ⅛ inch (3 mm)

templates

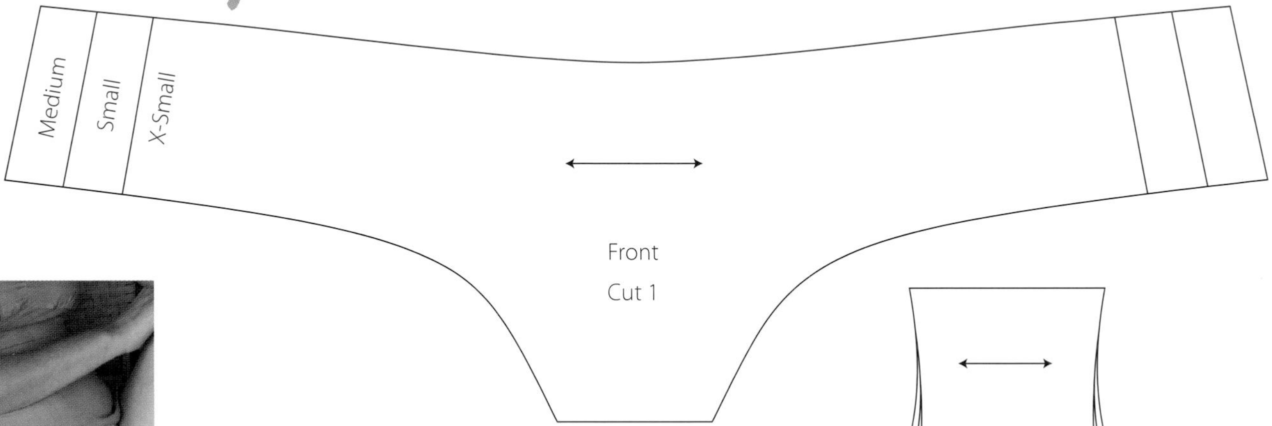

Front
Cut 1

Medium
Small
X-Small

Crotch
Cut 1 Stretch Fabric
Cut 1 Cotton Jersey

Medium
Small
X-Small

Narcissus, page 92
Enlarge 250%

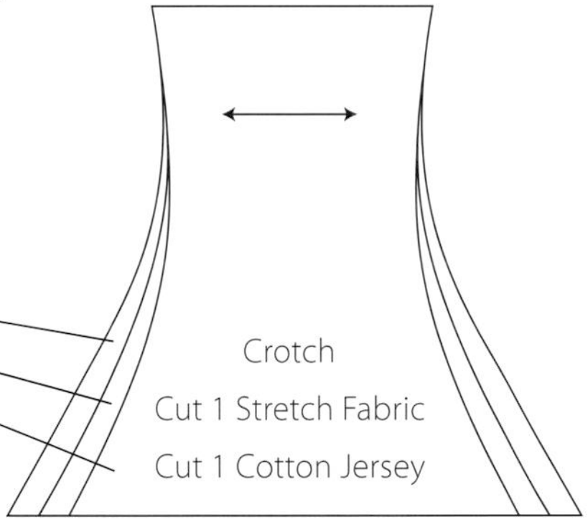

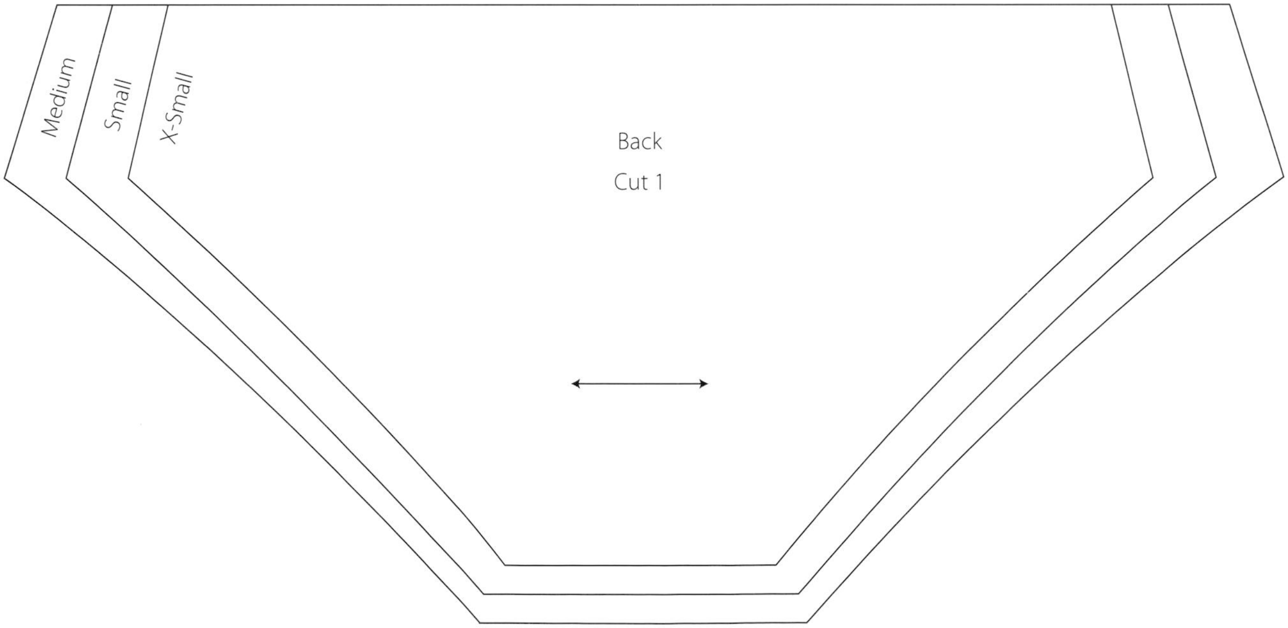

Back
Cut 1

Medium
Small
X-Small

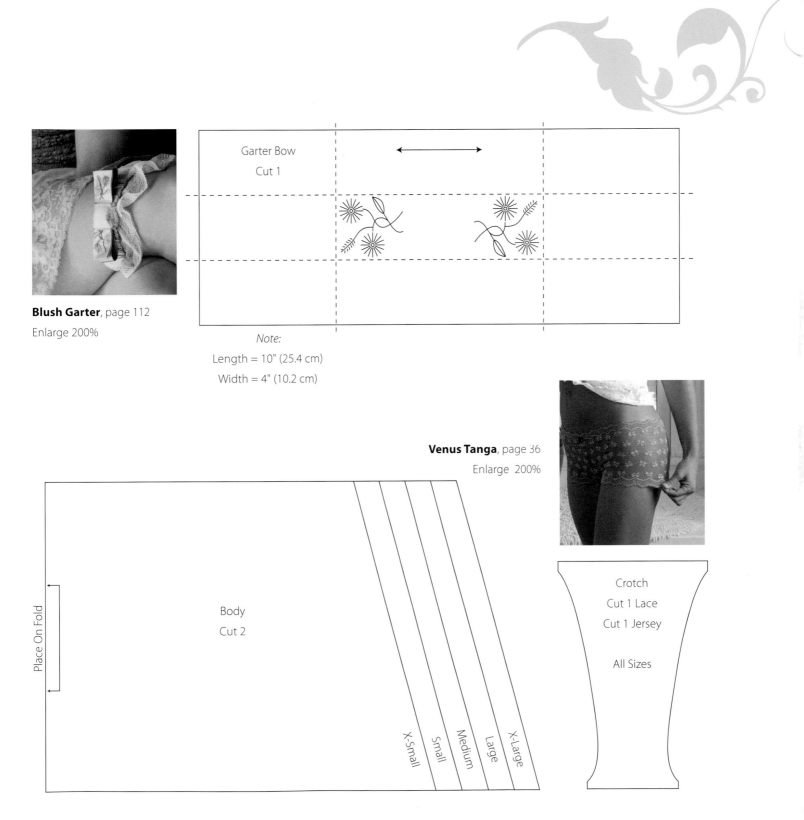

Blush Garter, page 112

Enlarge 200%

Garter Bow

Cut 1

Note:

Length = 10" (25.4 cm)

Width = 4" (10.2 cm)

Venus Tanga, page 36

Enlarge 200%

Place On Fold

Body

Cut 2

X-Small

Small

Medium

Large

X-Large

Crotch

Cut 1 Lace

Cut 1 Jersey

All Sizes

Medium

Small

X-Small

Body
Cut 2

Medium

Small

X-Small

Crotch
Cut 1 From Stretch Lace
Cut 1 from Cotton jersey

Sugarberry, page 114
Enlarge 250%

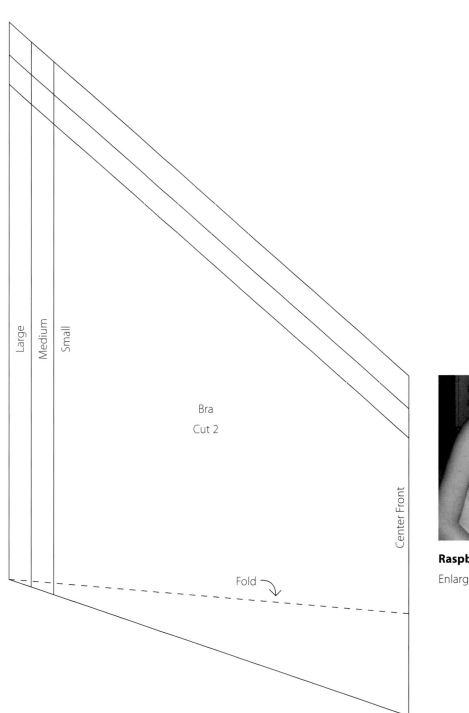

Large

Medium

Small

Bra

Cut 2

Center Front

Fold

Raspberry Swirl, page 57

Enlarge 125%

X-Large

Large

Medium

Small

X-Small

Back

Cut 2

outside leg seam

inside leg seam

Heartbreaker, page 80

Enlarge 300%

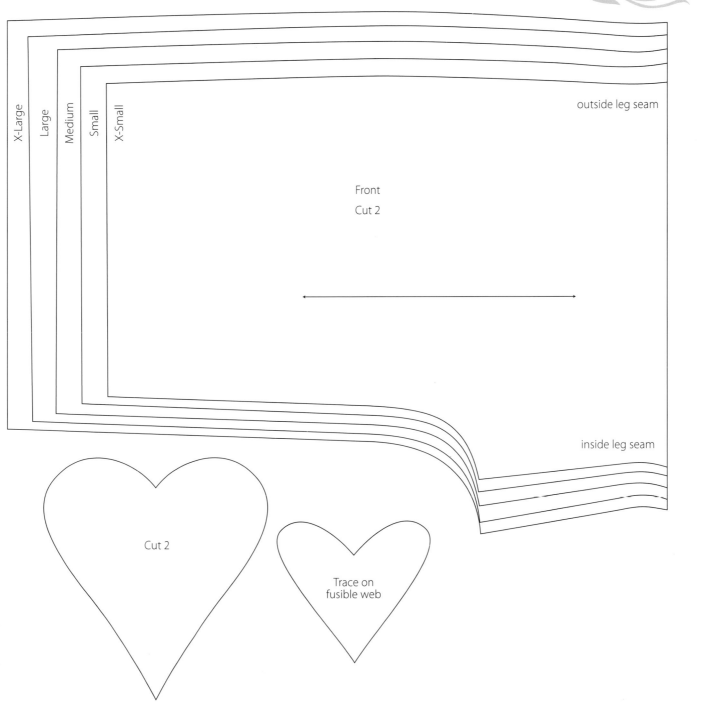

X-Large
Large
Medium
Small
X-Small

outside leg seam

Front
Cut 2

inside leg seam

Cut 2

Trace on
fusible web

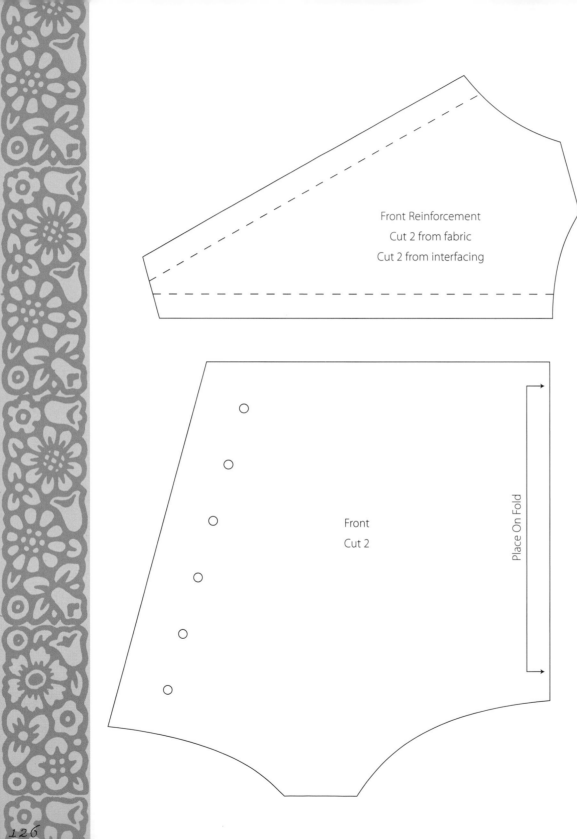

Front Reinforcement

Cut 2 from fabric

Cut 2 from interfacing

Front

Cut 2

Place On Fold

Girlesque, page 99

Enlarge 200%

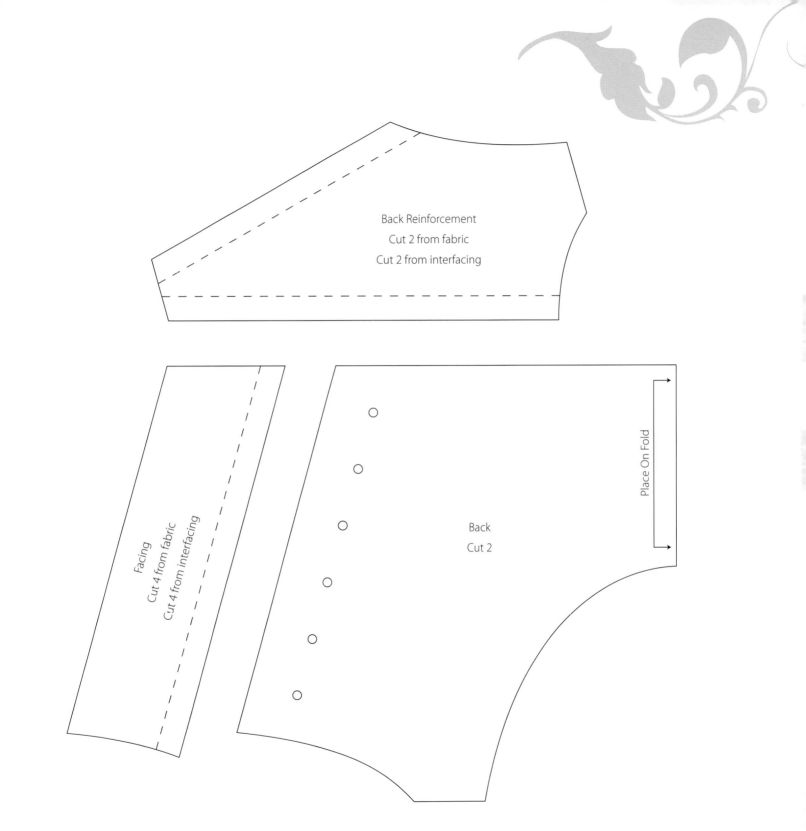

Back Reinforcement

Cut 2 from fabric

Cut 2 from interfacing

Facing

Cut 4 from fabric

Cut 4 from interfacing

Back

Cut 2

Place On Fold

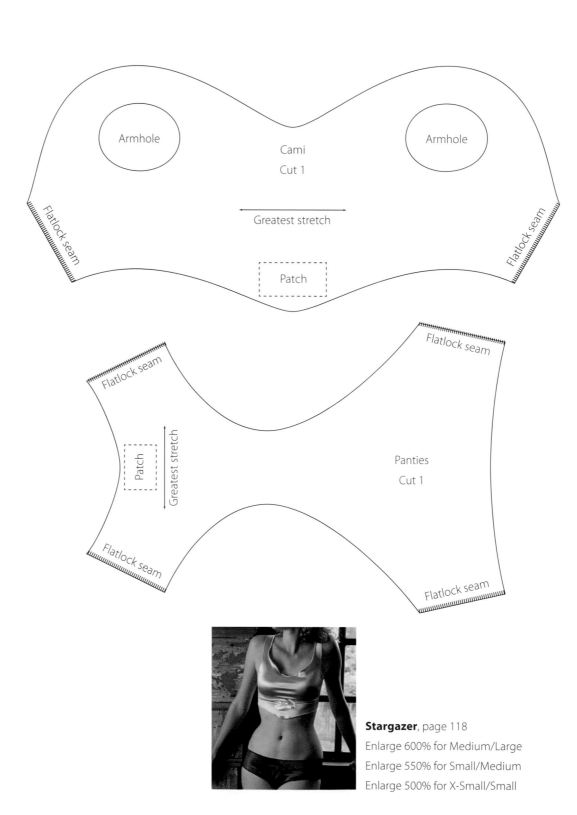

Armhole

Cami
Cut 1

Greatest stretch

Flatlock seam

Flatlock seam

Armhole

Patch

Flatlock seam

Flatlock seam

Patch

Greatest stretch

Panties
Cut 1

Flatlock seam

Flatlock seam

Flatlock seam

Stargazer, page 118

Enlarge 600% for Medium/Large

Enlarge 550% for Small/Medium

Enlarge 500% for X-Small/Small

about the designers

Justina Blakeney is a designer, a crafter, the DIY editor at *Venus Zine*, and a three-time published author. Her articles, tutorials, and illustrations have appeared in a wide variety of international publications and programs, including *The Today Show*, *Martha Stewart Morning Radio Show*, *Glamour*, Thread-bangers.com, Metro.pop, and Supernaturale.com. Justina loves watercolors, pesto, clay, big buttons and small details, birdcages, velour, bicycles, and veggie burritos. She co-owns Compai, a crafty, green design studio. Visit her anytime at www.compai.com.

As a designer and an author, **Janis Bullis** has been serving the fashion and interior design industry for more than 25 years. Her clients include book, magazine, and pattern publishers, as well as textile manufacturers. Janis has contributed to hundreds of how-to publications with designs ranging from eveningwear and children's costumes to window treatments and bed coverings. Her overall goal is to help people enjoy the benefits and rewards of creative sewing. Janis writes and sews in New York's beautiful Hudson Valley.

Alison Campbell grew up fascinated by history, castles, and big frocks, and she has always enjoyed sewing and hand embroidery. Alison loves giving new life to vintage lace and fabrics and turning forgotten treasures into something new to be cherished. She lives in Glasgow, Scotland. Pay her a visit through her Etsy shop, CrikeyAphrodite.etsy.com, or contact her directly at crikeyaphrodite@gmail.com.

An avid crafter since childhood, **Lisa Cox** attributes her passion for sewing, needlecrafts, and quilting to her mother and grandmother, who taught her the basics and encouraged her to develop her own style. Her designs have been featured on WhipUp.net and SewMamaSew.com and will be included in the Lark book *Pretty Little Presents* (2009). A rehabilitation consultant by day and crafter by night, Lisa lives in a coastal suburb of Perth, Australia, with her husband, David, and their children, Brenton and Sarah. Lisa and Sarah collaborate on the popular blog, A Spoonful of Sugar (www.spoonfullofsugar-girls.blogspot.com), where you can follow their crafting and baking adventures.

San Francisco native **Amara Felice** moved to New York in 1994 to learn accessories and millinery design at the Fashion Institute of Technology. Five years later she found a few like-minded women designers to partner with and opened Eidolon, a cooperative boutique featuring clothing, accessories, and gift items for women. Amara works out of her nearby studio, where she hand-produces accessories, lingerie, swimwear, and clothing. Check out Eidolon's website at www.eidolonbklyn.com.

Loretta Gjeltema is the co-creator of Kid's Sew Creative, a program for teaching sewing to children. Her work has been featured in both *Threads* and *Sew Stylish* magazines, and she is an active member of the Nashville Chapter of the American Sewing Guild, which she served as the founding president. You can visit her website at www.fittingtips.com or follow her ongoing sewing pursuits on her blog at www.fittingtips.wordpress.com.

Fiona Hesford studied at Brighton University, where she gained a degree in fashion and textiles; she has worked as a textile designer ever since. Her designs have been featured in *Elle Decoration* and *Marie Claire* magazines and in the Lark books *Pretty Little Presents* (2009) and *Pushing the Envelope* (2009). Fiona has created a collection of handmade products for the home that can be seen on her website at www.girls-institute.co.uk. She lives in West Sussex, England, with her artist husband, her twins, Alfred and Matilda, and her cat, Madame Mabelline.

Joan K. Morris's artistic endeavors have led her down many successful creative paths, including ceramics and costume design for motion pictures. Joan has contributed projects for numerous Lark books, including *Extreme Office Crafts* (2007), *Cutting-Edge Decoupage* (2007), *Pretty Little Pin Cushions* (2007), *Button! Button!* (2008), *Pretty Little Pot Holders* (2008), *50 Nifty Beaded Cards* (2008), and many more.

Elise Olson lives in Asheville, North Carolina, where she creates fun and sexy lingerie that is comfortable enough for a woman to wear every day. She sells these in boutiques and online at www.ontheinside.etsy.com. She can be reached by e-mail at elise_olson@yahoo.com.

Coming from a background of concentrated studies in the fine arts, **R. Brooke Priddy** applies her technical abilities in drawing and design to the dressmaking arts. Brooke started her handmade underwear label, Ship to Shore, in New York City in 2000, and soon broadened to include swimsuits and dresses. She now resides in Asheville, North Carolina, where she creates one-of-a-kind custom gowns and wholesales her handmade dresses and dainties to boutiques. For more information on Ship to Shore and Brooke's designs, visit www.shiptoshoreshop.com.

Lauren Scanlon is a studio artist living in Asheville, North Carolina. She holds a master of fine arts in printmaking and has exhibited her work across the United States. Lauren is the recipient of numerous awards, including the Duensing Scholarship, the Letterpress Residency at Penland School of Craft (2008), and an Artist-in-Residence award from the Vermont Studio Center (2008). For more information and images of her work, visit www.laurenscanlon.com.

Valerie Shrader made a pair of pink culottes when she was 11 and has loved fabric (and sewing) ever since. She is a senior editor at Lark Books, and has written and edited many books related to textiles and needlework. Valerie knits every now and then, too, and dreams about dyeing fabric and making artful quilts when she's not watching birds.

When **River Takada-Capel** was a little girl, her mom and dad spoiled her with all things handmade—from nightgowns, birthday cards, and backpacks. She learned how to make clothing by taking apart garments from thrift stores, and has enjoyed sewing her own clothing ever since. In particular, River loves reincarnating old clothing into something new and wearable. Take one peek in her closet, and you'll see it's overflowing with collaged pieces assembled from vintage Tee shirts, polo shirts, and dresses. River is a student at Haywood Community College in Clyde, North Carolina, where she studies traditional and professional crafts, and is honing her skills in fibers, weaving, sewing, dying, and printing. You may find River at one of the many craft shows she attends around the country. In Asheville, her wrap skirts can be found at Rags Reborn (www.ragsreborn.com).

acknowledgments

This book is all about sweet nothings, but our gratitude speaks volumes. A big shout out to all the designers for their passion and creativity. We couldn't have done it without you! Thank you to models Kia, Morgan, Melody, Melissa, Katie, and Crystal for making the projects all the more beautiful, and to Amanda Anderson for the stunning hair and makeup. Thank you to Kimberly Rollin, Fran McDermott, John and Annie Ager, Drs. Heather Spencer and Charles Murray, and to Mose and Terri Bond for letting us frolic in such gorgeous settings.

Lynne Harty is a goddess with a camera, and we can't thank her—or the talented art director, Dana Irwin—enough for presenting the projects in such a lovely light. Bernadette Wolf's illustrations really hit the sweet spot, and production editor Nathalie Mornu and her assistant, Kathleen McCafferty, lavished a great deal of attention on all things editorial. Thanks to writers Peggy Bendel and Nancy Wood for making the manuscript sparkle; editorial intern Jacob Biba and managing art director Shannon Yokeley, put the icing on the cake.

It's all on www.larkbooks.com

Can't find the materials you need to create a project?
Search our database for craft suppliers & sources for hard-to-find materials.

Got an idea for a book?
Read our book proposal guidelines and contact us.

Want to show off your work?
Browse current calls for entries.

Want to know what new and exciting books we're working on?
Sign up for our free e-newsletter.

Feeling crafty?
Find free, downloadable project directions on the site.

Interested in learning more about the authors, designers & editors who create Lark books?

index